PASSAGES
Study & Workbook

Pruning You for His Glory
AMY SLOSS

PASSAGES
Copyright © 2024 by Amy Sloss

All rights reserved. Neither this publication nor any part of this publication may be reproduced or transmitted in any form or by any means, electronic or mechanical, including photocopying, recording or any information storage and retrieval system, without permission in writing from the author.

Unless otherwise indicated, scripture quotations are taken from THE HOLY BIBLE, NEW INTERNATIONAL VERSION®, NIV® Copyright © 1973, 1978, 1984, 2011 by Biblica, Inc.® Used by permission. All rights reserved worldwide. • Scripture quotations marked (NLT) are taken from the Holy Bible, New Living Translation, copyright ©1996, 2004, 2007 by Tyndale House Foundation. Used by permission of Tyndale House Publishers, Inc., Carol Stream, Illinois 60188. All rights reserved. • Scripture quotations marked (ESV) are taken from The Holy Bible, English Standard Version® (ESV®), copyright © 2001 by Crossway, a publishing ministry of Good News Publishers. Used by permission. All rights reserved.

ISBN: 978-1-4866-2470-6
eBook ISBN: 978-1-4866-2471-3

Word Alive Press
119 De Baets Street Winnipeg, MB R2J 3R9
www.wordalivepress.ca

Cataloguing in Publication information can be obtained from Library and Archives Canada.

My wife and I are grateful to have participated in *Passages*. I can recommend this material for lots of reasons, but the three main ones are Amy's courage to share her story, her willingness to share with others what God has revealed to her, and her focus on scripture and worship throughout the study. There will be benefits and fruit for anyone who undertakes the study, and more blessings still for those with the faith to apply what they learn.

—Rev. Ryan Tudor, Senior Pastor, Owen Sound Alliance Church

Few books stirred my heart and challenged my walk with the Lord like *Passages* did. It called me to a raw honesty not just with myself, but with those people closest to me and ultimately with my Lord. I could feel God start to change my heart as I faced the honest (and sometimes ugly) truth, and as I started to live child-like into what He called me to become. *Passages* is about in-reach before outreach. It's about changing me so I can live radically—the way Jesus lived a life full of grace and love—with those around me. You won't study *Passages* just once but multiple times!

—Gisela Roux, child of God, wife and mother

Passages is a powerful resource packed with Biblical teaching and relatable examples. Through raw and unabashed personal anecdotes, Amy invites us to examine ourselves as she gently guides and inspires us to seek the Lord in all we do. I came away craving a deeper understanding of who God is, and with a desire to bring my behaviour into alignment with God's Word. This study will enrich your life.

—Rhonda Clark, Christian

Amy has a gifted way of being transparent about the journey God has taken her on so far in life as a wife, a parent, and an individual. I have walked through *Passages* as a participant as well as a facilitator. In both roles, I've been stretched and challenged to dig deeper and reflect on unresolved past and present issues, some I wasn't even aware resided within my heart! As Amy walks us through her story, we are reminded that even though our stories and struggles are different, we are the same—sinners in need of our Saviour, Jesus Christ. Understanding why we need to be set free from the pain and hurt allows for growth and an even deeper relationship with our Creator. Such a beautiful thing!

—Krista Cameron, mother of two and a daughter of the Most High

I wholeheartedly endorse *Passages* for its profound impact on personal growth, its emphasis on authentic relationships, and its ability to draw us closer to Jesus. Through this study, I have experienced the transformative power of God's presence. Whether you come as a woman of deep faith or someone searching for more authentic connections, this study will undoubtedly bless you. It opens doors to meaningful relationships within a small group, and it provides the fertile ground for God to work in your life, leading you to a deeper understanding of His love and purpose for you.

—Ange Torrie, sister in Christ

PASSAGES
Study & Workbook

STUDIES

PASSAGES

pas'sage - the act of passing from one place to another[1]

A shoot will come up from the stump of Jesse; from his roots a Branch will bear fruit.
(Isaiah 11:1)

Pruning You for His Glory

To my husband, Michael—for your support, encouragement,
and grace in giving me space to walk this journey.

Our children—Sarah, Rachel, Calvin, Nathan, and Wesley.
God uses you to teach my heart. You are each a perfect gift.

And to the Lord, for showing me one step at a time who I am and whose I am.
Give God all the glory!

Contents

FOREWORD	xiii
ACKNOWLEDGEMENTS	xv
INTRODUCTION	xvii
ABBREVIATIONS FOR THE BOOKS OF THE BIBLE	xix

The Root of Bitterness
SESSION ONE: LISTENING — 1

The Vine of Pride
SESSION TWO: CONTENTMENT — 17

The Branch of Judgement
SESSION THREE: SOUND JUDGEMENT—WISE MIND — 33

The Branch—Leash of Control
SESSION FOUR: SELF-CONTROL — 51

The Covering of Shame
SESSION FIVE: COMPASSION & HOPE — 61

The Branches of Idolatry: What Gives You Shape?
SESSION SIX: EYES ON THE LORD — 77

The Branches of Self-Sufficiency
SESSION SEVEN: CONFIDENCE IN SUBMISSION — 89

The Ice of Fear
SESSION EIGHT: THE MELTING OF FORGIVENESS
THE FEAR OF THE LORD — 105

The Soil of Jealousy
SESSION NINE: HE IS JEALOUS FOR ME — 119

Hate
SESSION TEN: WITH AN OVERFLOW OF LOVE — 131

A NOTE TO THE LEADER — 143

ENDNOTES — 145

BIBLIOGRAPHY — 145

ABOUT THE COVER ARTIST — 147

Foreword

If you had told me twenty-five years ago as a young stay-at-home mom and pastor's wife that my husband, Jim, and I would be missionaries providing biblical counselling and pastoral care, I never would have believed you. My personal testimony is one of rebellion, doubt (in myself and God), and times of severe depression from a very young age. I certainly didn't have it all together and was not and still am not your typical "pastor's wife." So needless to say, I didn't feel adequate or qualified to speak into lives or to be used by God. Isn't it amazing that as we mature in our faith, we realize that it's *in* and *through* our trials and weaknesses that God uses us the most! When we are weak, He is strong!

Water's Edge Ministries was born out of a deep love and concern for God's children. We saw a great need for biblical counsel and pastoral care in the church community, and it has been our privilege to sit with hundreds of couples, individuals, pastors, and ministry leaders over the years. It's our joy to listen, pray, encourage, and to wait on the Lord with expectation as He does the work of conviction, repentance, forgiveness, and healing of hearts!

What an honour to be asked by my dear friend Amy to write the foreword to *Passages*. I asked her to be a part of a Bible study I was hosting. Through this study and the two years that followed, Amy welcomed me into a very difficult season in her life. We spent many hours together sharing, laughing, crying, and praying. I'll never forget when she spoke these words out loud for one of the first times: "I think God wants me to share what He's been doing in my life with others, maybe in a study format!" Amy walked in faith and trusted God, and I'm so grateful that she did. What a blessing!

Passages has been in my life personally, as I still deal with the sin patterns of my heart. I continue to pray Psalm 139:23–24: *"Search me, God, and know my heart; test me and know my anxious thoughts. See if there is any offensive way in me, and lead me in the way everlasting."* I have used the biblical truths found in this study and have seen the fruit in many lives. I'm thrilled now that you too can move through the "passages" in your life as you listen to God's voice and allow Him to expose, prune, cleanse, regrow, and heal your hearts one step at a time! I know that Amy's humble prayer is for this study to point not to her but to our Holy God, abounding in love and mercy, able to do all things, gentle and faithful, forgiving, and compassionate!

My prayer is that as you work through this study alone or with a group, that you stand secure on the truth of God's Word and, like a drink for your thirsty soul, it refreshes you by the Holy Spirit as He reveals God's love and grace to you in a new way.

PASSAGES

The faithful love of the Lord never ends!
His mercies never cease.
Great is his faithfulness;
his mercies begin afresh each morning.
(Lamentations 3:22–23, NLT)

Sharon Nolson
Water's Edge Ministries
Owen Sound, Ontario

Acknowledgements

I am so thankful for each person God has brought into my life to help me on this journey. He really sent a whole army! I am grateful to Michael for saying yes to getting help with me and supporting and encouraging me each step of the way.

I'm thankful for our counselling sessions with Jim and Sharon, and for my sister in-law Dr. Christine Sloss, who connected us to her psychology clinic with Dr. Carmen Lalonde, who worked with us so patiently. I'm thankful for friends who walked alongside and prayed with me, and family that listened to my journey and continued to love and support us.

I'm grateful for my friend Dana, who was the first person I shared *Passages* with, and who shared her raw drawings for all to see and painted the cover. Thank you to each person who was willing to listen and be a part of *Passages* when I really didn't know how to explain what I was sharing. I appreciate each person's willingness to be open and share their story; it was such a special time with each of them. I'm grateful to Rhonda and Donna for sitting with me as we went through each word at a time as they helped me with their editing expertise. And I am thankful to Word Alive Press for helping me take *Passages* from a duo-tang to a book.

I am filled with gratitude for our children and their continued love and forgiveness. It was a gift to go through *Passages* with each of them and share my heart, as they have seen it all, each through a different lens. I'm thankful for the healing we've experienced together. This makes it all worthwhile. Nathan, thank you for being willing to let me share our stories, especially the passage you were on and how God used you to teach me so much about myself.

Passages would be nothing without the Lord's leading. Thank You, Lord, for caring for my heart as You do for every single person. Thank You, Lord.

Introduction

This Bible study comes from my journey, which you'll read about in Session One. The biggest tool on my journey was God's Word. I used my NIV Application Study Bible and sometimes looked up words from an old 1959 dictionary my in-laws gave me. I learned the importance of understanding words and how powerful they are. When I struggled with a word I felt convicted on, I'd look in my concordance/dictionary at the back of my Bible and write out all the verses containing that word. In this study, I share verses that spoke to my heart. In some weeks I share my personal journal entries and study notes from my Bible that gave me greater understanding.

If you're studying *Passages* with a group, I suggest spending an hour and a half on each session, which will give time for your stories, thoughts, and prayers. Each topic includes a list of scriptures. You can look at a couple during the session or on your own.

Come and get comfortable with a hot water—my favourite—or drink of choice. As you go through the sessions, share whatever you feel comfortable with—where you've been, where you are right now, and what you hope for. This is a lifelong journey, and I'm thankful He's not finished with us yet!

Amy

Abbreviations for the Books of the Bible

(The NIV Application Study Bible Concordance)

Genesis	Gn	Isaiah	Is	Romans	Rom
Exodus	Ex	Jeremiah	Jer	1 Corinthians	1 Cor
Leviticus	Lv	Lamentations	Lam	2 Corinthians	2 Cor
Numbers	Nm	Ezekiel	Ez	Galatians	Gal
Deuteronomy	Dt	Daniel	Dn	Ephesians	Eph
Joshua	Jos	Hosea	Hos	Philippians	Phil
Judges	Jgs	Joel	Jl	Colossians	Col
Ruth	Ru	Amos	Am	1 Thessalonians	1 Thes
1 Samuel	1 Sm	Obadiah	Ob	2 Thessalonians	2 Thes
2 Samuel	2 Sm	Jonah	Jon	1 Timothy	1 Tim
1 Kings	1 Kgs	Micah	Mi	2 Timothy	2 Tim
2 Kings	2 Kgs	Nahum	Na	Titus	Ti
1 Chronicles	1 Chr	Habakkuk	Hb	Philemon	Phm
2 Chronicles	2 Chr	Zephaniah	Zep	Hebrews	Heb
Ezra	Ezr	Haggai	Hag	James	Jas
Nehemiah	Neh	Zechariah	Zec	1 Peter	1 Pt
Esther	Est	Malachi	Mal	2 Peter	2 Pt
Job	Jb	Matthew	Mt	1 John	1 Jn
Psalms	Ps	Mark	Mk	2 John	2 Jn
Proverbs	Prv	Luke	Lk	3 John	3 Jn
Ecclesiastes	Eccl	John	Jn	Jude	Jude
Song of Songs	Song	Acts	Acts	Revelation	Rv

The Root of Bitterness
SESSION ONE
Listening

My Story

When I got married at twenty, I was still young in my faith. I had become a Christian at nineteen and thought I knew how I *should* live, as I'd grown up in a Christian home.

It didn't take long for some fruit to start to grow in my heart—anger, bitterness, and resentment. On the outside I looked very happy and wore a big smile. And at times I was. But my heart of bitterness grew …

After being married for over twenty years, with five children (two adopted), Michael and I got some marriage counselling, as I felt broken and then completely shattered. At the time, I felt God speak to my heart: "Only I can make something beautiful out of these shattered pieces." I was sure He was going to change Michael, as the problems weren't my fault! *"Fix him*!" I'd demanded of God over and over throughout our marriage.

The following year, we could see that we needed more counsel. This time though, it was help in parenting. Something had to change. Again, not thinking it was me …

I wrote down this verse to put behind my sink.

> *Do not conform to the pattern of this world, but be transformed by the renewing of your mind. Then you will be able to test and approve what God's will is—His good, pleasing and perfect will.* (Romans 12:2)

I did long to be transformed and I prayed daily to know His good, pleasing and perfect will.

Four months into therapy, I felt God ask me to write about my journey. I was hesitant, as I am not a writer. And why would I do that? Then each day I would write out what we were being taught in therapy and take it to God's Word—messing up again and again and wanting to quit, but hearing His voice saying to keep going one step at a time.

The Lord started to expose *my* rotten tree that had grown. I remember the day when I felt God speak into my heart, telling me that I wasn't fruitful … at all. I remember feeling so empty, vulnerable, and mad. Like, "Really, God? I'm a good Christian girl. I've worked hard, I do the right things, and I read my Bible *every* day!"

As I grumbled to God, I felt the air in my lungs disappear, then His breath started to fill up my lungs again. I knew I was being disciplined by God. I had a feeling in my heart and belly that's hard to explain. This emptying … that was good, uncomfortable … and I felt hurt and sad … yet hopeful. Over time, God showed me that I'd been a "wolf in sheep's clothing"—a fraud. I didn't even know.

On this journey, the Lord has shown me *who* I am and *whose* I am. I prayed over the years that I would love better, grow in wisdom, and have all the fruit of the Spirit, but it just wouldn't stick.

PASSAGES

I wanted good fruit to grow! But it couldn't grow on *my* branches. It was impossible, so God started chopping. With each chop, I would grieve for the impact that I'd had on my family. I thought it was out of love. I had been deceived.

Each time I wanted to pick up my chopped branches and hold them on, because I felt it was too hard to trust God. He was asking me to trust Him and let go, one step at a time He would show me a different way.

After seven months of writing, I felt God ask me to reread what I'd written, and He said that there would be ten sessions from my journey. I was keen and excited to get going, as I really wanted to share what the Lord was teaching me. I tried to come up with topics along the way as I was reading, but I felt God say, "Wait."

I felt convicted to be baptized, as I'd questioned over the years if it was the right thing for me to do. I was baptized when I was twelve with a few people in my Sunday school class. At that time, I remember feeling so ashamed and embarrassed, wondering why I was doing it. With the chopping the Lord had done in my heart, I didn't want to be ashamed of Christ in me. Now I wanted to be baptized out of obedience.

Through writing my testimony, God gave me a picture of all the branches He had pruned—really my whole tree. Then He showed me what He wanted to grow in me instead, but *only in His strength*. I'm sharing about the branches that were chopped off, the root system that needed to be replaced, the soil that needed to be cleansed, and the planks that needed to be removed. I'll share about what He exposed and the new branches He has begun to grow in my heart from Him.

I felt like I was a seasoned Christian, and it was those around me who God needed to change. Instead, God showed me how much He loved me and cared about my heart. He wanted to restore me, showing me where I'd conformed to the patterns of this world, and then He wanted me to *be* transformed by the renewing of my mind. At that point, I'd be able to test and approve what God's will is—His good, pleasing, and perfect will.

This is vulnerable and not easy, yet His work in our hearts and minds for Him is the best thing we can live for. It's an honour to share my story and journey with you.

Your sister in Christ,
Amy

Pray

Have someone open in prayer. Thank God for your story and where you've been. Pray that you will listen and have an open heart to what the Lord wants to say to you.

Chop—Bitterness

As I shared in my story, God showed me that *bitterness* was my root system, and He wanted to renew my mind. "Bitterness" is the first word we're going to work through. I've included several questions, and I encourage you to answer the ones that you can, and if you would rather not, that is okay too.

How would you define bitterness?

_____
_____
_____

What is the difference between bitterness and anger?

_____
_____
_____
_____

What has been the impact of bitterness in your life?

_____
_____
_____

Would someone close to you describe you as a bitter person?

_____
_____

> *My dear brothers and sisters, take note of this: Everyone should be quick to listen, slow to speak and slow to become angry, because human anger does not produce the righteousness that God desires. Therefore, get rid of all moral filth and the evil that is so prevalent and humbly accept the word planted in you, which can save you.* (James 1:19–21)

What stands out to you in the above verse?

_____

_____

_____

Study Notes for James 1:19

When we talk too much and listen too little, we communicate to others that we think our ideas are much more important than theirs. James wisely advises us to reverse this process. Do others around you feel like they are heard and have value?[2]

Study Notes for James 1:19, 20

These verses speak of anger that erupts when our egos are bruised—*"I am hurt"; "My opinions are not being heard."* When injustice and sin occur, we *should* become angry because others are being hurt. But we should not become angry when we fail to win an argument or when we feel offended or neglected. Selfish anger never helps anybody.[3]

Wrestle

My anger was brewing 99 per cent of the time, because I was continually offended. I must have quoted this verse a thousand times to our kids: *"Everyone should be quick to listen, slow to speak and slow to become angry"* (James 1:19). That's all I focused on, yet I wasn't leading by example. I had justified my anger because I was *right,* yet it led to bitterness. God exposed my human anger and selfish anger, but I really wanted to produce the righteousness that God desired. Convicted in my heart, I could see that the two could not co-exist.

Is it hard for you to *listen*?

_____
_____

Are you quick to become angry?

_____

What makes you angry?

_____
_____

Do you feel justified in your anger?

_____

Next comes His instructions: "*Therefore, get rid of all moral filth and the evil that is so prevalent and humbly accept the word planted in you, which can save you*" (James 1:21).

What would be considered "*moral filth and evil*"?

_____
_____

Do you think that bitterness is evil?

_____

Can you think of a biblical story in which bitterness led to evil actions?

_____
_____
_____

Describe a time when God's Word "saved you"?

_____
_____

Grow—Listening

God gives instructions on how to work through the anger that is ready to erupt, or the bitterness that wants to smolder. The antidote is to listen. First, *listen* …

I filled up the *space* of our home with words, with an atmosphere that was more like a *"resounding gong"* (1 Corinthians 13:1). The Lord was asking me to give space in my heart, mind, and home for Him. That required me to do less talking. My *many* words were affecting my relationship with my husband, our children, and ultimately, the Lord.

What is filling up your space, your thoughts, and your surroundings?

_____
_____
_____
_____

We use a phrase in therapy called "riding the wave." It means to give space for the other's emotions and your own. Instead, I wanted to cut off the emotions by giving instructions, saying a verse, reprimanding, and disciplining, thinking I was helping. I knew God was asking me to listen, even in the storm. And to start, I needed to talk less! And *listen* …

Validating

In therapy we talked a lot about *validating*. I realized that I *gave* a lot of non-validating statements, like, "What were *you* thinking?" or "You don't need to be so angry!" or "What is the matter with you?" Oh, there are many more! I also sent non-validating messages in non-verbal ways, such as rolling my eyes and walking away.

Some examples of validating statements could include, "Tell me more about what happened" or "That sounds really frustrating." Maybe saying nothing at all at that moment is validating. I was learning the importance of helping a situation instead of hindering it. I had and will have many opportunities to practise this skill.

List two or three non-validating statements or postures.

_____

_____

_____

List two or three validating statements or postures.

_____

_____

_____

When have you *not* felt heard? How did that impact you?

_____

_____

_____

What is the impact of *not* feeling heard?

_____

_____

_____

When we listen, we're saying, "I hear you, I care, and I value you." Even if you *don't agree* with what's going on. Listening gives space for the situation.

How has God shown you that He is *listening* to you, or how has He shown you your value?

_____

_____

_____

PASSAGES

Scripture

Choose a verse on bitterness, anger, or listening and describe how it speaks to you.

BITTER(NESS): having a taste that is sharp and unpleasant; expression of severe pain, grief, or regret[4]

| Prv 14:10 | Prv 27:7 | Eph 4:31 | Heb 12:15 |
| Prv 17:25 | Rom 3:14 | | |

ANGER, ANGRY: a strong feeling of displeasure or hostility

Ex 15:7	Nm 32:10	Ps 2:12	Prv 15:1
Ex 32:10-12	Dt 9:19	Ps 30:5	Prv 29:22
Ex 32:19	Dt 29:28	Ps 78:38	Prv 30:33
Ex 34:6	Jgs 14:19	Ps 86:15	Jon 4:2 (Jonah)
Lv 26:27-28	2 Sm 12:5	Ps 90:7	Mt 5:22
Nm 14:18	2 Kgs 22:13	Ps 95:10	Eph 4:26
Nm 25:11	Neh 9:17	Ps 103:8	Jas 1:19

LISTEN(ED)(ING)(S): to hear; to pay attention

Dt 30:20	Prv 18:2	Mt 12:42	Acts 3:22
1 Sm 3:9 (1-18)	Prv 18:13	Mk 9:7	Jas 1:19-22
1 Kgs 4:34	Is 66:4	Lk 10:39	1 Jn 4:6
Neh 8:3	Ezk 2:5	Jn 10:27	
Prv 12:15	Dn 9:6		

Why is it hard for you to listen?

_____

_____

_____

_____

> *Why do you look at the speck of sawdust in your brother's eye and pay no attention to the plank in your own eye? How can you say to your brother, "Let me take the speck out of your eye," when all the time there is a plank in your own eye?* (Matthew 7:3–4a)

I came on this journey with a huge plank in my eye, thinking everyone *else* needed to change. Yet the Lord started to show me my sin. He started chopping and showed me my plank. He then was able to use that plank to start building a bridge to the people in my home. When we look at the speck in someone else's eye, we can't build anything out of that. This is really a self-evaluation. God wants our whole heart, but the urge is to point and say, "What about them?"

What spoke to your heart today?

_____

_____

_____

_____

After each session there is a suggestion of a song to listen to. You can look up the songs on YouTube, Spotify, or another music sharing site. After the song, I encourage you to pray and share what God has been speaking to you, if you feel comfortable.

Song: "Nothing Else" by Cody Carnes

Prayer: Thank God for what He has shown your heart today.

Look over life-work.

Explaining Life-Work/Homework

I encourage you to take time each day with the Lord. I call this your life-work. Look up one or more verses from the lists of words from each session, but *please* don't feel overwhelmed with this. These aren't exhaustive lists, and there might be other verses not on the list that speak to your heart.

When a verse speaks to your heart, think of or write down what the verse is speaking to you about. *Listen* to what God wants to say to you. Often it's good to look at the context of that verse. I encourage you to read above or below and see what's going on.

It's really a "choose your own adventure." I know God wants to speak to your heart. If one scripture speaks to your heart and you are changed, then that's amazing! Soak in that one verse for the whole week or longer. That is the power of Christ in you.

Journaling isn't for everyone, but give it a try and maybe you'll like it. Maybe you're a visual learner and can draw what each of the key words mean (i.e., *bitterness* and *listening*). No art skill required! My friend Dana was willing to share the raw drawings she drew when she took the course. God is so personal. It's encouraging to know when God is speaking to our heart. It builds our faith and encourages others.

When we want to grow in the Lord, the enemy doesn't like it! Sometimes it can feel more frustrating, agitating, uncomfortable, and sad when our hearts are being exposed. This isn't easy, and being vulnerable is hard.

During the sessions, I say "fleshing it out" a lot. It comes from the following verse:

> *So I say, walk by the Spirit, and you will not gratify the desires of the flesh. For the flesh desires what is contrary to the Spirit, and the Spirit what is contrary to the flesh. They are in conflict with each other, so that you are not to do whatever you want. But if you are led by the Spirit, you are not under the law.* (Galatians 5:16–18)

God asks us to get rid of what our "flesh" wants, which is the world's way. Instead, we're to desire the way of the Spirit. There is constant tension in that. God asks us to renew our minds. May you be encouraged as you seek Him.

—Amy

Life-Work

1. Prayer for the week.

2. Write down or think of your story.
    Reflect on where you've been, where you are today, and what you hope for in Him.

3. Reflect or ask.
    Reflect on your life and where there has been a bitter root. If you're up to it, ask someone close to you if they can see bitterness in you.

4. Practice listening and giving space.
    Breathe in and out with no words. Give it a try and do it again.
    Speak a lot less this week. Listen to what is going on around you.
    Give space for the Holy Spirit to work in your heart and the hearts of others.

5. Try to validate someone around you each day.

6. Read scripture each day.
    On "bitterness", "anger", or "listening".

7. Journal or draw.
    Write the verse out and write down what God is saying to you in this verse. Note your questions, struggles, and joys.
    If you want, try drawing a picture of what bitterness, anger, and listening look like to you. We can learn a lot from a picture.

8. Share next week:

pas'sage - the act of passing from one place to another

Bitterness

"A figure. First, thorny vines of anger entangling her, twisting around her until they turn into bars of constraint (which is bitterness). She is trapped and cannot move. All the while, she is shouting to be heard, twisted."

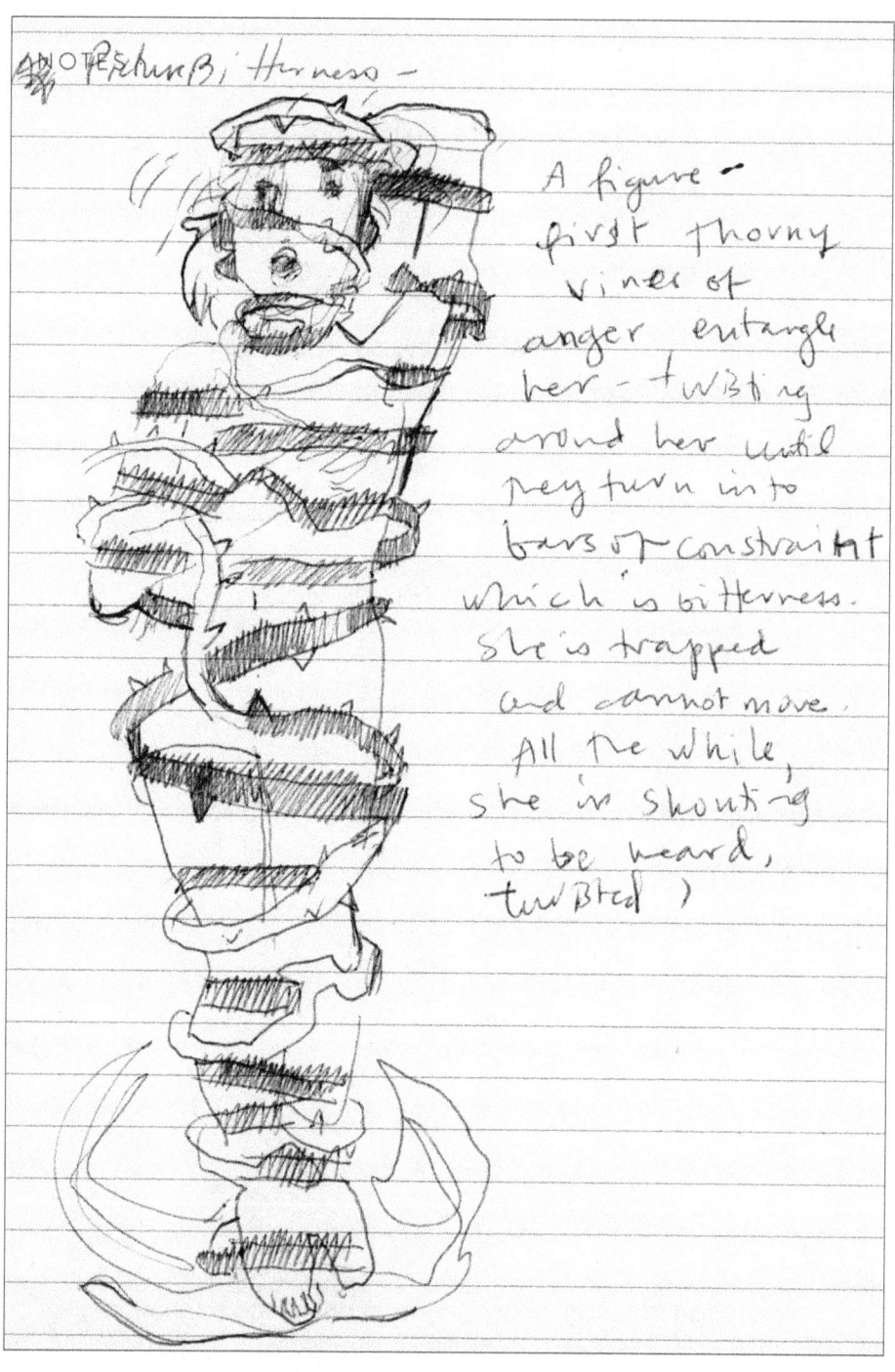

Listening

"Nurturing, time, patience, quiet, kindness, love, comfort."

The Vine of Pride
SESSION TWO
Contentment

 Welcome back, friend!

In our first session, we talked about anger, bitterness, listening, and validating.

Review

How was your week? *You may not need to ask all of the review questions.*

Were you able to think of your story? (Take a couple of minutes to share.)

How did you do at listening?

Were you able to talk less?

Could you recognize any bitterness in yourself? Did you ask someone?

Did any verses or pictures speak to your heart this week? In what way did it speak to you?

Were you able to validate others? How?

Pray

Pray that you will listen and have an open heart to what the Lord wants to say to you.

Chop—Pride

This session is full, so take a deep breath. Looking into our hearts makes us vulnerable, and it's hard.

What would need to change in your life for you to have more peace in your heart?

_____

_____

_____

PASSAGES

What does pride or being proud look like to you?

_____
_____
_____
_____

Do you think that you struggle with pride?

_____
_____
_____
_____

Wrestle

I picture pride as a creeping vine that chokes out humility and then takes over. Through my bitterness, I grew a *healthy* vine of pride. Before this plank was exposed, if asked, I would have answered, "Well, maybe I do have some pride. Don't we all?"

I didn't think I was prideful, but then the Lord started opening my eyes and kindly showed me, in His gentle and loving way, that I was prideful. I just thought I was living the "better" way. If others changed, *then* I would be happy and have more peace in my heart, mind, and life!

My eyes were focused on what I thought others should change, and I saw others' weaknesses as failures. This perspective made me mad, resentful, angry, and bitter—even hateful. My heart over the years spewed venom. At the same time, I was also singing praise to Jesus through songs like "I Surrender All." I was thinking in my heart that I was justified in my actions.

An example of this appeared in my parenting. When our eldest was around twelve, she said to me, "Mom, you expect me to be perfect." I didn't think that; I just wanted her to do the *right thing*. That was my job as a Christian mom: correct, discipline, instruct, repeat. Memorize scripture, pray, repeat again. Out of love and being obedient to God, I thought I was doing the right thing.

The environment that grew in our home from my *pride* and rules grew hostile. I thought it was out of love, but I was deceived. When my eyes were opened to the truth, I could see the destruction my sin of pride had caused. That stung my heart. I grieved it. God was showing me a different way.

Scripture

In session one, we looked up a verse in each section and you shared what you felt God was saying in the verse. You can complete this section with others or leave it for your life-work.

PRIDE: an excessively high opinion of oneself; conceit

| Prv 8:13 | Prv 29:23 | 2 Cor 7:4 | Jas 1:9-10 |
| Prv 16:18 | Is 25:11 | Gal 6:4 | |

PROUD: arrogant or haughty; having excessive self-esteem

| Ps 101:5 | Prv 16:19 | 1Cor 13:4 | Jas 4:6 |
| Prv 16:5 | Rom 12:16 | 2 Tim 3:2 | |

HUMILITY: the state of being humble; lack of pride

Ps 45:4	Prv 22:4	Phil 2:3	Jas 3:13
Prv 11:2	Zep 2:3	Col 2:18	1 Pt 5:5
Prv 15:33	Acts 20:19	Col 2:23	
Prv 18:12	2 Cor 10:1	Col 3:12	

> *Then we will no longer be infants, tossed back and forth by the waves, and blown here and there by every wind of teaching and by the cunning and craftiness of people in their deceitful scheming. Instead, speaking the truth in love, we will grow to become in every respect the mature body of Him who is the head, that is, Christ. From Him the whole body, joined and held together by every supporting ligament, grows and builds itself up in love, as each part does its work.* (Ephesians 4:14–16)

What stands out to you in this verse?

_____

_____

I did feel tossed back and forth in the waves! As a wife and mom, I was sure I had loved others by speaking the *truth in love*. But I had this sharp conviction while reading Ephesians 4:15 that I loved more out of *rules in love*. If you followed my rules, all would be well.

I couldn't see that before that moment! I wept and apologized to Michael. As I shared with him my convictions, he right away told me, "Yes, you have conditional love." That stung my heart. I told him that this was just a self-evaluation—I wasn't asking for his opinion!

Throughout our marriage, Michael never felt that he was *good enough.* Then in my parenting style, I passed that on to our children—the idea that they needed to be perfect and follow my rules. The vine of *pride* crept into those relationships. *Rules without love* is not love at all.

I was filled with pride, thinking that *my way* was better. And I couldn't accept anything but my way. God exposed my prideful heart, yet He did it in such a way that broke me, and then He filled me by showing me His way. This took time to understand and then time to live out.

Can you think of an area in your life where you feel "tossed back and forth"? You want to go one way, but you act another way?

_____

_____

_____

Have you thought about the way you love others? How would you describe that?

_____

_____

_____

Radical Acceptance

In therapy, we use the phrase *radical acceptance*, which means accepting the situation around you, even if you don't agree with it; for example, "I accept that you are struggling right now" or "I accept that I don't know all the answers and need to get help."

I really struggled with radical acceptance. It actually made me mad, because I'd think, *How am I to accept that*?

What would be an example of radical acceptance?

_____

_____

_____

THE VINE OF PRIDE

What is something that is hard for you to accept in someone else or yourself?

_____

_____

_____

To the Bible to work this out!

> *But He said to me, "My grace is sufficient for you, for my power is made perfect in weakness." Therefore, I will boast all the more gladly about my weaknesses, so that Christ's power may rest on me. That is why, for Christ's sake, I delight in weakness, in insults, in hardships, in persecutions, in difficulties. For when I am weak, then I am strong.*
> (2 Corinthians 12:9–10)

What stands out to you in this passage?

_____

_____

_____

_____

This verse was transformational! It opened my eyes, and I understood that it wasn't for me to carve out others' weaknesses. Yet it made me mad, because I didn't like it. I had to read this over and over again. The truth was, I hated others' weakness. I hated the insults; I hated the hardships. Was I being persecuted? I felt so! I wanted all my difficulties to go away! Looking back on this attitude, I can see how childish it was to always want my own way. How I wanted to mature! As described in Ephesians 4:14–16, I felt like I was in a huge wave being tossed back and forth. I wanted it to stop! But I had to learn to *ride the wave* and allow God to show me His truth.

"*But He said to me, 'My grace is sufficient for you, for my power is made perfect in weakness'*" (2 Corinthians 12:9). In this verse, God showed me that if His grace is sufficient for me, His grace is sufficient for my husband and children.

In my *rules in love*, I wasn't giving grace; I was saying "*change now.*" I was irritated when they didn't change. In my *pride*, I thought I knew what was best for them. "Follow *me*! Right now! Or else!" Yikes!

PASSAGES

Can you believe that His grace is sufficient for you? *This is not an easy question*

_____
_____
_____

Can you believe this for others?

_____
_____
_____

Can you believe and have faith that "His power is made perfect in weakness" for you?

_____
_____
_____

Often this can be hard to believe for difficult people close to your heart. Can you believe and walk in faith that this is true for them?

_____
_____

What makes this hard to live out?

_____
_____
_____
_____

What is one of your weaknesses?

_____
_____

Re-read 2 Corinthians 12:9–10 on page 25.

What would it look like to boast or delight in yours or others' weaknesses, insults, hardships, persecutions, and difficulties?

___

___

___

How does this encourage you? *"For when I am weak, then I am strong."*

___

___

___

___

When we experience God's strength through our weakness, this gives the glory to God, not to me and not to you.

My heart softened. If the Lord wants to do that for me, He also wants to do that for my husband and my children in their weaknesses too.

Again, I needed to apologize. I was trying to use my fairy godmother's magic wand and not giving space, not listening, and not seeing their weaknesses as opportunities for the Lord to show His power. I was *not accepting* them for who they are. God showed me such a different perspective. I was learning to trust that He was and is using the weaknesses of myself and others. This will continue to be fleshed out, I'm sure, for the rest of my life, as pride will want to sneak in.

> *… we also glory in our sufferings, because we know that suffering produces perseverance; perseverance, character; and character, hope. And hope does not put us to shame, because God's love has been poured out into our hearts through the Holy Spirit who has been given to us.* (Romans 5:3–5)

Do you like suffering?

___

PASSAGES

How has suffering produced perseverance, character, and hope in your life?

_____

_____

_____

Grow—Contentment

I wanted this beautiful picture of me with perseverance, strong character, and unwavering hope, but no suffering, as I was *not content* with my suffering. This was another example of feeling tossed back and forth in the waves! "Rules in love." I know I can't do that on my own strength.

I quoted this catchy verse to my kids over and over again—even put it to a song. But did I believe it for myself and live it out? No, I did not.

"*I can do all <u>this</u> through him who gives me strength*" (Philippians 4:13, emphasis added). What does *this* mean? It's so important to look at the rest of the scripture.

<u>Read Philippians 4:10–13 together.</u>

What gets in the way of you being content?

_____

_____

_____

What is the secret to being content?

_____

_____

_____

In what area of your life has God shown you His strength in your weakness?

_____

_____

_____

When a vine of pride is entangled around my mind and heart, I am trusting in my own strength, in my own way. I was learning to radically accept and be content with what God has given me. I was learning to be content with the situations God has entrusted me with.

I can do all this through him who gives me strength. (Philippians 4:13)

Scripture

Choose a verse and share what it's saying to you, or you can do this as part of your life-work.

WEAK(ER): frail; feeble; unable to withstand persuasion or temptation

Ps 41:1	Rom 14:1	1 Cor 8:9	2 Cor 12:10	Heb 12:12
Ps 82:3	Rom 15:1	1 Cor 12:21-22	1 Pt 3:7	
Mt 26:41	1 Cor 1:25-27			

WEAKNESS(ES): shortcoming

Rom 8:26	1 Cor 15:43	2 Cor 12:9	2 Cor 13:4	Heb 4:15
1 Cor 1:25				

STRENGTH(EN)(ENED)(ENING): capacity for endurance

Ex 15:2	Ps 73:26	Is 40:31	Eph 3:16
Dt 6:5	Ps 84:5	Is 41:10	Phil 4:13
1 Chr 29:12	Ps 118:14	Jer 9:23	Col 1:11
Neh 8:10	Ps 147:10,11	Hab 3:19	2 Thes 2:16,17
Ps 18:1	Prv 24:5	Mk 12:30	Heb 11:34
Ps 28:7	Prv 30:25	Lk 22:32	Heb 12:12
Ps 46:1	Is 31:1	1 Cor 1:25	
Ps 59:17	Is 35:3,4	Eph 1:18,19	

CONTENT(MENT): to be pleased, satisfied, willing; satisfaction

Jos 7:7	Prv 19:23	Phil 4:11,12	Heb 13:5
Jb 36:11	Eccl 4:8	1 Tm 6:6	
Prv 13:25	Song 8:10	1 Tm 6:8	

PASSAGES

What spoke to your heart today?

_____

_____

_____

_____

_____

Song: "Closer" by Brandon Lake

Prayer: Thank God for what He has shown your heart today.

Look over life–work.

> *Do not conform to the pattern of this world, but be transformed by the renewing of your mind. Then you will be able to test and approve what God's will is—his good, pleasing and perfect will. (Romans 12:2)*

Life-Work

1. Prayer for the week.

2. Write out or think about where you wish you were.

3. "Brag" about each person in your family.
   Reflect on their strengths privately or share with someone else.
   Remember to brag about yourself too.

4. Acknowledge your weaknesses and those of your family members.
   You could also ask them what they think their weaknesses are. This might feel uncomfortable, but it helps us to see and understand each other. We all have weaknesses.

5. Read scripture, journal, and/or draw each day.
   On "pride," "humility," "weakness," "strength," or "content."

6. Radically accept and be content.
   Try to acknowledge an area in your life in which you're not content. What is God asking you to radically accept and be content with?

7. Continue to listen and validate.

8. Share next week.

pas'sage - the act of passing from one place to another

Pride

"What I have drawn beside the sketch: angry at people who don't care. I care so much, but it's my own perspective. Thought of injustice. Anger with others, angry thoughts. I'm blindfolded (in my own head). Wondering why people are so unkind. I don't trust anyone. Looking at life through my own lens."

Humility

"Deflation: A modest or low view of one's own importance. I see this as a humble position; offering to help someone in small and big ways is putting oneself into a humble posture. In the picture, God showed me someone sitting lower and offering her shoes to someone who is in need of shoes. We can all offer help by listening and caring. Lowering ourselves/putting our needs aside to help another. Not thinking of oneself."

The Branch of Judgement
SESSION THREE
Sound Judgement—Wise Mind

Welcome back, friend.

There was a lot of work to do last session as we looked at pride in our lives, humility, weaknesses, and truth in love. We also talked about radical acceptance and contentment. Pride is a stubborn vine that the enemy delights in.

Review

How was your week?

Was any pride revealed to you?

How did it feel to brag about your family and yourself?

How did it feel to reflect on your own and your family's weaknesses?

Did any verses or pictures speak to your heart?

Did you identify any areas of your life where you aren't content?

Were you able to radically accept or be content with something?

Pray

Pray that you will listen and have an open heart to what the Lord wants to say to you.

Song

Today we will begin with a song if you want. Rest your heart and mind as you sit and listen to "Do it Again" by Elevation Worship.

Has it ever felt like God has failed you? My honest answer to this is "Yes, it sometimes does feel like God has failed me." It seemed as though He wasn't listening to me! He wasn't doing what I wanted Him to do. And I was not radically accepting or being content in where I was. I would listen to this song "Do It Again" and weep because I felt like God had failed me.

PASSAGES

Chop—Judgement

This week we're working through judgments given and received and the impact of that.

What does the word *judgement* mean to you?

_____

_____

_____

What is the difference between being *prideful* and being *judgemental*? How do they work together?

_____

_____

_____

_____

Pride: an excessively high opinion of oneself; conceit.[5]

Judgement: to pass sentence upon; condemn; to act or decide as a judge; to form a negative opinion about; good sense; the final judgment of God.[6]

Read Luke 10:38–42 together. —"The Little Sister Spat."

How is bitterness present in this story?

_____

_____

_____

Where do you see pride in the story?

_____

_____

_____

What judgement is being passed and by who?

___

What do we learn about listening?

___

If you can picture yourself as a Martha, what would Jesus be saying to you?

___

Wrestle

I didn't know I was so judgemental. Chop! That's another branch needing to come off! The Lord showed me that I was judging others, which put up barriers in my relationships. I sometimes got so angry, yet I was trying to live the right way. This is another example of how I felt tossed back and forth. I was mad at other people who weren't doing things my way!

Pride and judgement were working together to grow the *bitterness* in me.

In some of the sessions, I share bits of my daily journal writing. This week I am sharing what my thoughts were when wrestling with judgement and after reading the story of Mary and Martha.

Passages—My Daily Journal Writing

Yesterday, I was mad that the enemy has had so much room in my heart for so long. As I was crying out to the Lord, I asked the question, "Why didn't You rescue me on all those occasions that I was calling out to You?"

I hear in my heart, "I was, Amy. I was there all along, guiding you as I am guiding you now."

"Why did it take me so long to understand?" I ask.

"Because I wanted all of you."

"I thought I was giving You all of me."

"I know you did ... just like Martha thought that she was giving all of herself. This is how patient I am with you. I am showing you this now so you can show the same patience with those around you."

"Really?"

"Yes, Amy. Listen to My voice.

"Thank You, Lord, for the peace You have given me, and for how You are for my heart."

I had made demands of God because I wanted to write out my story, and the stories of those around me, my way.

Are there judgements you heard about yourself as a child, teen or adult that have stuck with you for a long time? Even today?

_____

_____

_____

_____

_____

THE BRANCH OF JUDGEMENT

What has been the impact of that on your life?

_____
_____
_____
_____

How do judgements affect people?

_____
_____
_____
_____
_____

A couple of judgements I felt as a child were:

I was told that I was scatter-brained. I know I was and am still. I also struggled in school, so I believed that I wasn't smart. Those judgements became part of my identity and led me to conclude that I didn't have value. God has shown me that those judgements don't define who I am. And now I'm able to see that He uses those things in me. Only God could do this!

Read together Matthew 7:1–5

Any thoughts from that scripture?

_____
_____
_____
_____
_____

I wanted to make it all about me, as my eyes were looking at others and how they impacted me. But God wanted me to look at my own heart. It felt too hard. It was so much easier to see other people's specks!

Scripture

Choose a verse and share what it's saying to you, or you can do this as part of your life-work.

JUDGE(D)(S): judging to pass sentence, punish or condemn; one appointed to do this

Gn 16:5	Prv 24:23	Mt 7:1-5	2 Cor 10:7
1 Sm 24:12	Prv 29:14	Jn 7:24	2 Tm 4:1
1 Chr 16:33	Is 33:22	Jn 12:47	Heb 12:23
Ps 51:4	Jer 11:20	Acts 17:31	Jas 3:1
Ps 75:2	Ezk 7:27	Rom 2:16	Jas 4:12
Ps 82:8	Ezk 34:17	Rom 14:10	Rv 20:12
Ps 96:13	Mi 3:11	Gal 2:6	

JUDGEMENTS: to pass sentence upon—condemn—to act or decide as a judge, to form a negative opinion about; good sense, the final judgment of God

Dt 1:17	Jer 25:31	Acts 24:25	1 Pt 4:17
1 Sm 25:33	Hos 6:5	Rom 2:1-3	2 Pt 3:7
Ps 119:66	Mt 10:15	Rom 11:33	1 Jn 4:17
Prv 3:21	Mt 12:36	Rom 12:3	Jude 1:6
Prv 18:1	Jn 9:39	Rom 14:10,13	Rv 14:7
Eccl 12:14	Jn 12:31	2 Cor 5:10	
Is 53:8	Jn 16:8	1 Tim 3:6	

Wise Mind/Truth in Love

In therapy, we worked through a strategy called *emotion mind* and *fact mind*, with the goal of a *wise mind* in the middle sharing both of those qualities. As I would share my perspective of a situation, our psychologist would say, "What are the facts?" I would feel a grumble in my heart, as I felt justified in my perspective. Our psychologist was showing me how I was responding with my emotional thoughts and actions.

What we hear and what's being said and communicated can often get lost in the interpretation and translation of the *emotion mind*. It was important for me to sift through what I *thought* was the truth—"rules in love"—and grow into "truth in love" by renewing my mind. I was learning to differentiate the emotions from the facts in situations, and then responding with wisdom.

Let's work this through.

What is the impact on others and ourselves if we only function in the emotional mind?

_____
_____
_____

What decisions in the Bible were made with the emotion mind?

_____
_____
_____

What is the impact on ourselves and others if we just function in the fact mind?

_____
_____

Share an example of when you responded or made a decision using either the fact mind or emotion mind.

_____
_____

Grow—Sound Judgement

This verse has helped me gain greater clarity about judgement: *"My son, do not let wisdom and understanding out of your sight, preserve sound judgment and discretion; they will be life for you, an ornament to grace your neck"* (Proverbs 3:21–22).

When I respond with just an emotion mind or a fact mind, I don't use sound judgement. I can be quickly offended, sharp-tongued, and annoyed while feeling justified in my response as I follow the flesh.

When we have wisdom and understanding, we can have sound judgement and discretion.

I had a hard time gaining clarity and not jumping to my emotion mind. I needed to flesh it out, to understand it. I was blind to the judgements I had of others.

Passages: My Daily Journal Writing

(This is a long one.)

I'm feeling deflated again, wondering how to keep going. What am I to write? I absolutely love the insight I got from the Lord, and it still feels like the biggest challenge to put it into practice—to be transformed in Him.

Having my girls away. I miss them. I know I'm not as needed, and that's a good thing. The role of a mother. Wondering what you would have me write about, Lord? I feel scattered and lost for words. Lord, what's going on? Stop thinking about me?

I know I'm often self-absorbed, annoyed, because "What about me?"

Tonight as I got off Facetime with Sarah and Rachel, I had many feelings. Sarah doesn't seem engaged in talking with me. She doesn't ask how I'm doing; it doesn't feel like she needs me.

Rachel is having fun and can't chat.

Michael isn't reading my "writing" that I asked him to read, as I want to share with him.

Calvin gives me dirty looks.

Nathan thinks my goal is to make him angry.

Wesley is yelling at me.

ME, Me, me. How do I think less of me? Is this what it comes down to? Not thinking about myself? I feel led to:

Do nothing out of selfish ambition or vain conceit. Rather, in humility value others above yourselves, not looking to your own interest but each of you to the interests of the others. (Philippians 2:3–4)

I'm feeling encouraged, with His life-giving breath in my heart and lungs. That's right, it isn't about me. Oh, how I long for it to be! That's what gets in the way so often—ME, ME, ME! My feelings are hurt. I can't do this anymore. I am angry. I, I, I! Just another verse of the same song! Could I really live any differently?

This is speaking to my heart, as I feel lighter. We're told to take care of ourselves, stay regulated so we can help others be regulated. Take care of me first! No?

But seek first his kingdom and his righteousness, and all these things will be given to you as well. Therefore do not worry about tomorrow, for tomorrow will worry about itself. Each day has enough trouble of its own. (Matthew 6:33–34)

Jesus is talking about worry, and when I'm concerned about me, I'm worrying, "What about me?".

Look at the birds of the air; they do not sow or reap or store away in barns, and yet your heavenly Father feeds them. Are you not much more valuable than they? Can any one of you by worrying add a single hour to your life? (Matthew 6:26–27)

"*Are you not much more valuable than they?*" Oh, how that speaks to my heart. Even though I am to put others first, I feel so treasured by God. He sees me as valuable, even if I don't feel that from my family at times. I know I'm having a little pity party with just me invited. I know I am valued by my family, but by their actions, I wasn't feeling valued in one way or another.

Because I didn't overly connect with Sarah on Facetime, I assume she must not need me, and I don't feel valued by her, as she's not asking about me.

Truth—Sarah had a full week of exams and volunteering. Her head space is full, she's hungry, and she's wondering what she'll be doing next.

Rachel was having fun and couldn't chat. I must not be needed or valued.

Truth—I truly am happy for her. I love seeing her happy.

Michael isn't reading my writing. He must not think this is important, or value me.

Truth—He's had a full day of serving me by building closets for Rachel's room, as it was on my list of things for him to do before Rachel comes home. He would like to read it. Give him space and time. He asked me to remind him, and he will read it. He loves me so much.

Calvin's creative eye-rolling makes me think he must not value me.

Truth—Calvin had a busy day at work and doesn't need my motherly words of wisdom at this time.

Nathan—Oh, the tension he brings me! Does he even care what I say, think, and feel?

Truth—He values me, even when it doesn't look like it. He treasures our family and thinks he has a happy, loving home.

Wesley is yelling at me, so he must not value me either.

Truth—Wesley is also tired from our active day; he longs for a gentle response from me every time.

When I'm thinking of myself and my own perspective, I can become emotion-minded. It seemed a bit dreadful when I read this verse: "To put others first." It made me feel: "What about me?" And here I go. I just need to die to myself … again.

I believe God is bringing an adjustment in my thinking. Seek Him first. He values me sooo much. *"Are you not much more valuable than they?"*

Seek Him first, and I'll be able to "see" others around me through a different lens.

"But seek first His kingdom and His righteousness, and all these things will be given to you as well."

When I am confident in my value from Him, I'm able to see His truth and trust Him in that. I can listen to my children without being offended and bothered as much … right? When Michael isn't doing what I want him to do, I can trust that he values me for who I am without getting my way. I can share my thoughts, share who I am, and not be afraid. Oh, how this would change my thinking, my actions, my heart, my life!

… but be transformed by the renewing of your mind … (Romans 12:2).

Emotion and fact mind, when working well together, bring "Truth in Love"—God's way. Clarity. How I want it to be "All About Me!"

(You made it through!)

Any thoughts from that long journal entry?

_____

_____

_____

What can make it challenging to value others above yourself?

_____

_____

_____

Do you see yourself as valuable? This can be a hard question.

_____

_____

_____

Describe a time when you judged a situation but then learned the facts and saw that you'd been wrong once you had a better understanding and sound judgement.

_____

_____

_____

    This is my story about judging our son and the impact it had on me and my perspective of him. I call it "The Baby Porcupine Story."

    I was sharing one of our situations from the week during our parenting therapy session. I told our psychologist that I had asked Nathan to go outside to give each of us space, as we'd had a big conflict. He went behind the house, and then I could see him staring me down through the window, like a tiger ready to devour me. I moved in front of the fireplace so he couldn't see me. He proceeded to move around the house to the other side so that he could see me through another window. He was looking at me just as intently.

"He was like a tiger that wanted to devour me!" I was looking for sympathy, and it was a cry for help!

Right away she said, "No, he's not a tiger. He's just a baby porcupine with his quills up."

I then tried to state my case again, as I knew she didn't understand my situation. I invited her for the weekend so she could see for herself!

Again she told me, "Oh no, he's just a baby porcupine."

We closed the computer down after our session, as it was online because of COVID. Michael and I scoffed at each other, confirming that she didn't know what she was talking about. If she only lived with us, she could see that she could be eaten too!

That afternoon I was going to get a book to read to Wesley from our stack of books from the library. Then I saw it—a book titled *Baby Porcupines*! I knew this was from the Lord! I didn't even remember getting the book. The Lord was showing me through our psychologist, and now confirming it from the library, that Nathan was just a "baby porcupine." I needed to adjust my thinking! Really? A baby porcupine? I then emailed her a picture of the book and told her that the Lord was using her to show us the truth today!

As a parent, my perception of my situation in our home became skewed as I felt out of my depth and thought I didn't have the skills to save him or myself! That's a bit over-dramatic, I know. Often my reaction was based on history or fear of the future, instead of being present right in the moment. I needed to get to know him, not just for how I *thought* I saw him. Over time, this helped heal our relationship, because I got rid of my judgements. This allowed me to see Nathan through a different lens.

I had clothed myself with assumption. My judgments led to destruction. I made statements like "He's annoying me! He's so bad. He's making me so frustrated!"

Our therapist asked us over and over, "What are the facts?"

When I could look at the facts and have understanding, I could have sound judgement, wisdom, and walk by the Spirit. I was very comfortable with my "Mom Judge Badge." But God wanted to chop it off, and He was showing me another way.

> *My son, do not let wisdom and understanding out of your sight, preserve sound judgment and discretion; they will be life for you, an ornament to grace your neck.* (Proverbs 3:21–22)

THE BRANCH OF JUDGEMENT

What spoke to your heart today?

_____

_____

_____

_____

_____

Song: "Something Has to Break" by Red Rocks Worship

Prayer: Thank God for what He has spoken to your heart today.

Look over life-work.

> *Do not conform to the pattern of this world, but be transformed by the renewing of your mind, then you will be able to test and approve what God's will is—His good, pleasing and perfect will.* (Romans 12:2)

PASSAGES

Life-Work

1. Prayer for the week.

2. Look at a situation or conflict in your life.
    Did you respond with the emotion mind?
    Look at the facts and ask God for the truth.
    How did that change your perspective?

3. Acknowledge areas in which you have felt judged.
    Write down any judgements you felt as a child, teen, and/or adult.
    Beside each one, write out the facts surrounding it.
    Then write out the truth about each judgement.
    What is God saying to your heart? Take your time. "Truth in Love."

4. Read scripture, journal, and/or draw each day.
    On "judge" or "judgments."

5. What is God asking you to radically accept and/or be content in?

6. Continue to listen and validate.

7. Share next week.

pas'sage - the act of passing from one place to another

Judgement

"My ideas are better, self-destruction, obliviousness, anger, pointing the finger, diminishing, puffing myself up, I'm better than you. Sketch: Wearing a sort of childish outfit. Helmet of righteous ideas. Binoculars that are looking outside instead of at their heart. Pointing the finger. Robe with lightning bolt. They're covered up. Feet stuck in the mud—can't get out of a judgmental pattern."

Wisdom/Sound Judgement

"Peace, calmly waiting, reading a book, the train goes by—I don't react."

The Branch—Leash of Control
SESSION FOUR
Self-Control

 Hello, friend, and welcome back.

Last time, we talked about our judgements and the need for His sound judgement. We discussed emotion mind, fact mind, and wise mind. Truth in love.

Review

How was your week?

Did you see areas where you passed judgement or felt judged?

Did you have a conflict this week that you were able to look at through a different lens?

Was there a moment when you were in emotion mind but then could look at the facts and have a wise mind?

Did any verses or pictures speak to your heart?

Pray

Pray that you will listen and have an open heart to what the Lord wants to say to you.

Chop—Control

This week we're discussing temptation and control. Transitioning to a new topic can be hard. It's okay if nothing comes to your mind.

What's one temptation you struggle with?

_____

_____

_____

_____

PASSAGES

How do other people's temptations affect you?

_____

_____

_____

Wrestle

The Lord showed me that my main temptation was to try and control others.

While hiking with my friend, she asked me if I had a "picture" to describe where I was at. I said that I could picture Nathan on the same beautiful, strong leather leash I had on our other kids. Around the handle loop were rivets that made the leash look really pretty. It was such a good leash, the best—so I thought.

As I transferred this leash to Nathan, I had a tight grip on it. To me, it was for an obvious reason—so he couldn't get away. I thought it was for his good, out of love. He needed my help to control the situation. But when I jerked the leash, he would look back, and the rivets looked like spikes. Then he would growl at me and want to "bite back." I wouldn't let go, and "out of love," I would bring it in tighter. I thought I was helping.

I knew God was asking me to get a retractable leash. I argued with Him: "Do you know how flimsy they are? He could cut it with a small knife." I was afraid to let go of *my* strong leash. I felt God encouraging me to let go of my leash and trust Him with this new wimpy leash. If I did that, it would give both of us more breathing space, and I would be letting go of control and trusting the Lord.

So many times over the years, God asked me to trust Him. I would say "yes," but my actions said, "*No*, I can't let go. I must control."

A month later, I was in the kitchen looking out my window, and I felt God speak to my heart. "No leash." It spoke to the core of my heart. What? No leash? I knew that was what God was asking me to do. He wanted me to let go of the leash, as there are no verses in the Bible that say, "Have your children on leashes." Not one.

God knew I couldn't handle going from my super snazzy leather leash to *no* leash. I needed to grow in trusting Him. That's how much He cares for my heart.

The truth was, I wanted things to go my way. I was beginning to understand that the leash was a form of control.

What are you trying to control?

_____

_____

_____

How is wanting or trying to control working in your home or in your heart?

_____

_____

_____

How is it affecting your relationships?

_____

_____

_____

> *You hypocrites! Isaiah was right when he prophesied about you:*
> *"These people honor me with their lips,*
> *but their hearts are far from me.*
> *They worship me in vain;*
> *their teachings are merely human rules."* (Matthew 15:7–9)

My *rules in love* produced bitterness and pride and led to my desire to control. This verse showed me that I was honouring Him with my lips, but my heart was far from Him. That stung my heart.

What is something that you have struggled with over and over again?

_____

_____

Can you have grace for others when they fall into temptation?

_____

_____

PASSAGES

What makes this hard?

_____

_____

_____

Read Matthew 4:1–11 together.

Study Notes for Matthew 4:1

> The time of testing showed that Jesus really was the Son of God, able to overcome the devil and his temptations. A person has not shown true obedience if he or she has never had an opportunity to disobey. We too will be tested. Because we know that testing will come, we should be alert and ready for it. Remember your convictions are only strong if they hold up under pressure.

When reading this it made me feel "grumpy."

> Jesus wasn't tempted inside the temple or at his baptism but in the desert where he was tired, alone, and hungry, and thus more vulnerable. The devil often tempts us when we are under physical or emotional stress (for example, lonely, tired, weighing big decisions, or faced with uncertainty). But He also likes to tempt us through our strengths, where we are most susceptible to pride. We must guard at all times against attack.[7]

What can make you feel vulnerable?

_____

_____

_____

_____

Looking back on my "leash" example, I realized I was *vulnerable* from my experiences with Nathan's weakness. I was *tempted* to tighten the leash! I thought it was best that I *controlled* the situation and the outcome, but the real outcome was frustration, lack of trust, and resentment. It eventually led to a breakdown in our relationship.

I wasn't trusting in the Lord. I was trusting in myself, thinking I was right and that I was trusting in the Lord! GRRRR! THE ENEMY!

> *Trust in the Lord with all of your heart*
> *and lean not on your own understanding;*
> *in all of your ways submit to him,*
> *and he will make your path straight.* (Proverbs 3:5–6)

Was I willing to let go of the leash? Was I willing to let go of the outcome? Was I willing to trust God's guidance? I longed for a renewal of my mind, so I had to say, "Yes—leash be gone!"

I am vulnerable, as the desire to control still creeps in, and I can quickly pick up the leash again. But my eyes were opened to the impact that control had and continues to have at times. The Lord in His patience would and will show me another way if I am listening. It is hard, but it's *so* much better.

> *Now faith is confidence in what we hope for and assurance about what*
> *we do not see.* (Hebrews 11:1)

When we can see and control the outcome, that is not faith.

"*The tempter came to him and said, 'If you are the son of God, tell these stones to become bread'*" (Matthew 4:3). Satan is called the tempter. It seems too hard to stand against him, yet "*I can do this through him who gives me strength*" (Philippians 4:13).

I am vulnerable when I'm not content. It was so hard and yet beautiful to see how God was showing His way. I have weaknesses. I am tempted. I am vulnerable. I want to control. Yet, *His power is made perfect through my weakness* (2 Corinthians 12:9).

Grow—Self-Control

<u>Read Galatians 5:16–25 together.</u>

Another "ah ha" moment! This was my Post-it note revelation as I tried and tried to have *all* the fruits of the Spirit. But it wouldn't stick if I was determined to be in control. This led to some of the acts of the sinful nature that are obvious and mentioned in Galatians 5. I just zipped by those verses and wanted all the fruits of the Spirit.

When I saw this, I was so frustrated with the enemy! Over the years, I have often quoted the "Fruits of the Spirit" verses of Galatians to the kids. Expecting—even at times demanding—that they must live this way! Children, *do it*! Again, I wasn't leading by example. Thankfully, God is showing His way, for His glory. That is amazing.

I love this part, as it's at the beginning and at the end of the passage (emphasis added):

> *So I say, walk by the Spirit, and you will not gratify the desires of the flesh.* (Galatians 5:16)

> &

> *Since we live by the Spirit, let us keep in step with the Spirit.* (Galatians 5:25)

When I can see the challenges in our home through the lens of weaknesses, I can see how we are all being tempted. There's a battle going on for our hearts. God asks me to "walk by the Spirit" with them.

I am weak, my husband is weak, and my children are weak. I'm being hypocritical if I look down on their weakness, where they have fallen into temptation, yet don't see how I fall into temptation as well. Sting.

Again, I wanted to use my fairy godmother magic wand and have things my way! God was helping me grow and trust in His way. Leash be gone! Only by the Spirit's power can I grow in His fruit of self-control and in His strength.

Scripture

Choose a verse and share what it's saying to you, or you can do this as part of your life-work.

TEMPTATION: to entice someone to sin; cause of enticement

Mt 4:1	1 Cor 7:5	1 Tim 6:9	Jas 1:13
Mt 6:13	1 Cor 10:13	Heb 2:18	
Mt 26:41	Gal 6:1	Heb 4:15	

SELF-CONTROL(ED): restraint exercised over one's own impulses, desires, or emotions; temperance

Prv 25:28	Gal 5:23	Ti 2:12 (1-12)	2 Pt 1:6
1 Cor 7:5	1 Tm 3:2		

What spoke to your heart today?

_____

_____

_____

_____

_____

Song: "Lord, I Need You" by Matt Maher

Prayer: Thank God for what He has spoken to your heart today.

Look over life-work.

"Do not conform to the pattern of this world, but be transformed by the renewing of your mind, then you will be able to test and approve what God's will is—his good, pleasing and perfect will." (Romans 12:2)

Life-Work

1. Prayer for the week.

2. Think of one thing you want to control.
    When are you vulnerable?
    What is your temptation?
    What is the outcome?

3. Picture control.
    If you were to think of a *picture* of control, what would that look like to you?

4. Read scripture, journal, and/or draw each day.
    On "temptation" or "self-control."

5. What is God asking you to radically accept and/or be content in?

6. Continue to listen and validate.

7. Share next week.

pas'sage - the act of passing from one place to another

The Covering of Shame
SESSION FIVE
Compassion & Hope

Hello, friend, you have made it to "halfway day!"

Last time, we talked about the desire to control, identifying our temptations, and then growing in self-control in His strength.

Review

How was your week?

Did you see areas where you have a "leash" of control?

How do you picture control?

Did you see any areas of temptation?

Did any verses or pictures speak to your heart?

Pray

Pray that you are listening and have an open heart to what the Lord wants to say to you.

Chop—Shame

This week we're talking about shame. Transitioning can be hard.

How would you describe *shame* or *ashamed*?

___

___

___

How is shame different from judgement?

___

___

PASSAGES

How do shame and judgement work together?

_____

_____

_____

Wrestle

When we talked about *shame* in our therapy session, I thought, *Now this is something that I do not struggle with. Finally!*

By the end of the session, though, I was convicted that shame was a form of communication that had grown full-blown in my mind and heart. I thought I was helping and showing love, but it was actually another branch of control. And the results were a whole covering of shame given and received in my life. How could I live any differently?

> *What is impossible with man is possible with God.*
> (Luke 18:27)

Only in the Lord's strength is it possible.

Passages—My Daily Journal Writing

While I wrestle with shame, I am led to John 9:1–5.

Being Washed

> *As he went along, he saw a man blind from birth. His disciples asked him, "Rabbi, who sinned, this man or his parents, that he was born blind?"*
>
> *"Neither this man nor his parents sinned," said Jesus, "but this happened so that the works of God might be displayed in Him. As long as it is day, we must do the works of Him who sent me. Night is coming, when no one can work. While I am in the world, I am the light of the world."* (John 9:1–5)

I've struggled with my struggles and wondered why. Are you listening to me, God? He must not be listening to me. I'm not asking for much! And all along God has been asking for all of my heart. My love was conditional, and that overflowed into how I loved my family. Again, not fruitful! (rules in love)

We're getting help with Nathan. I hope that this changes him, but I feel God opening my eyes. Nathan's struggle has opened my eyes to so much about myself. I'm getting to know who Nathan is, not who I want him to become. When I focus on who I want him to become, I miss out on the reason why: *"But this happened so that the works of God might be displayed in him."*

Again this speaks to me. Why do You "allow" pain and suffering? (Not a new question.) *"This happened so that the works of God might be displayed in him."* This is a lot for my brain to wrap itself around. When I don't see this, my heart can put shame on them for their weakness. NOT FRUITFUL! If someone was blind, I wouldn't shame them and put them down for that!

But I do shame Michael and our kids for not seeing what I see, expecting them to see what I see. Then pride and resentment breed like a wildfire. I'd even like to have a personalized license plate: "DUCWTIC" (Do You See What I See)

After saying this, he spit on the ground, made some mud with the saliva, and put it on the man's eyes. "Go," he told him, "wash in the Pool of Siloam" (this word means "Sent"). So the man went and washed, and came home seeing. (John 9:6–7)

Amazing! When the Lord heals us, it's not in the way we would have thought! Yet in my heart I can feel like, "Spit and mud? Yuck! Don't touch me with that! Heal me or others around me the way I want you to, Lord!"

His neighbors and those who had formerly seen him begging asked, "Isn't this the same man who used to sit and beg?" Some claimed that he was. Others said, "No, he only looks like him." (John 9:8–9)

Hearing people's testimonies is such a beautiful thing. With a stranger it's easy to believe. With a neighbour? They weren't sure. They knew the man. I think in our family it can be similar. "Was he *really* changed? Was he *really* healed? We'll see."

"How then were your eyes opened?" they asked. He replied, "The man they call Jesus made some mud and put it on my eyes. He told me to go to Siloam and wash. So I went and washed, and then I could see." "Where is this man?" they asked him. "I don't know," he said. (John 9:10–12)

Father, help me to know and understand You more. I pray that my perspective of what I see as struggles will change to *"This happened so that the works of God might be displayed in him."* When I get yelled or screamed at again and again, it's hard to see that it's going to be used for Your glory. Testing … *help me with my unbelief.*

Think of a struggle or challenge in your life: If you felt ashamed of it, what was the impact of that on you?

___

In what ways might you shame others?

___

THE COVERING OF SHAME

What was something you were "blind" to but God helped you see?

_____
_____
_____
_____
_____

What can get in the way of your eyes being opened?

_____
_____
_____

My heart was encouraged and strengthened after reading John 9:1–12. The Lord was helping me to see my heart and posture of shame, even though I didn't like what I saw.

Scripture

Choose a verse, and let's wrestle together with it. You can also do this as your life-work.

SHAME(D)(FUL): disgraced, humiliation, often at hands of an enemy

Ps 34:5	Prv 18:13	Rom 5:5	2 Cor 4:2
Ps 25:3	Jer 10:14	Rom 9:33	Heb 12:2
Ps 69:6	Jl 2:26	1 Cor 1:27	

ASHAMED: feeling of shame, guilt, or disgrace

| Mk 8:38 | Rom 1:16 | 2 Tm 1:8 | 2 Tm 2:15 |

Can shame be good? In what way?

_____
_____
_____

PASSAGES

How is our shame taken away?

_____
_____
_____

Share some examples of shaming statements. These are similar to non-validating statements. It could be said to others or even yourself.

_____
_____
_____
_____
_____

What are triggers to feeling shame?

_____
_____
_____

Possible triggers might include rejection, social humiliation, failure to meet expectations of others, bullying, trauma, labelling, criticism, judgement.

I wrote the following on the same night I felt exposed with shame in our therapy session.

Passages—My Daily Journal Writing

I was reading a missionary book that Rachel brought home from Bible school. I was peering over the book, annoyed and smirking in my heart as I looked at Michael on his phone. (I've had years of practice.) I felt in my heart that I was clearly using my time better by reading this missionary story.

I felt the Holy Spirit say, "Have compassion." It was so gentle that instantly my smirking ended, as I felt busted. I was filled with compassion. Wow!

I continued to read. The next paragraph of the story said, "He gave me something I'd never bargained for; compassion" (Bruchko, 27). I was in awe! The Lord was showing me very clearly that I need to have compassion. Smirking and shaming aren't of the Lord. Chop! Compassion—that is from the Lord! I know that in the story their compassion was much bigger than a phone disgruntlement!

If you had asked me if I was compassionate toward Michael, I would have said, "Absolutely ... maybe?" If you had asked Michael, I'm pretty sure he would have said, "Not really" or just a flat-out "no."

God was asking me to be compassionate. Would my actions follow that?

> ... faith by itself, if it is not accompanied by action, is dead. But someone will say, "You have faith; I have deeds." Show me your faith without deeds, and I will show you my faith by my deeds. You believe that there is one God. Good! Even the demons believe that—and shudder. You foolish person, do you want evidence that faith without deeds is useless?" (James 2:17–20)

Any thoughts to share?

_____

_____

_____

_____

_____

Grow—Compassion & Hope

As I looked at the verses on *compassion*, the Lord softened my heart. Again I needed to apologize to Michael and the kids for loving them with this distorted love through shame. Another example of my *rules in love*. Yet I would struggle over and over to trust in His way.

PASSAGES

<u>Read John 8:1–11 together</u>—The Woman Caught in Adultery

Why did the woman feel ashamed?

_____
_____

What impact did Jesus' compassion have on her?

_____
_____
_____

What hope did she have?

_____
_____
_____

Can you think of a time when someone showed you compassion when you did something wrong? How did that make you feel?

_____
_____
_____

Is it hard for you to have compassion with the people closest to you or with yourself? If so, why?

_____
_____
_____

> *...who redeems your life from the pit*
> *and crowns you with love and compassion.*
> (Psalm 103:4)

To wear a crown of love and compassion—that is a beautiful crown!

> *And hope does not put us to shame, because God's love has been poured out into our hearts through the Holy Spirit who has been given to us.* (Romans 5:5)

Scripture

Choose a verse and share what it's saying to you, or you can do this as part of your life-work.

COMPASSION(ATE): loving sympathy, empathy

Ex:6	Ps 145:8	Mt 15:32	Col 3:12
Dt 13:17	Is 54:10	Mt 20:34	Jas 5:11
Neh 9:17	Jon 4:2 (Jonah)	Rom 9:15	1 Pt 3:8
Ps 86:15	Zec 7:9	2 Cor 1:3	
Ps 103:4	Mt 9:36	Eph 4:32	
Ps 119:156	Mt 14:14	Phil 2:1	

HOPE(S): to desire something with confident expectation of its fulfillment

Jb 13:15	Ps 146:5	Rom 5:4	Col 1:27
Ps 25:3	Ps 147:11	Rom 8:20	1 Thes 1:3
Ps 33:17	Prv 13:12	Rom 8:25	1 Thes 5:8
Ps 42:5	Prv 23:18	Rom 12:12	Ti 1:2
Ps 62:5	Is 40:31	Rom 15:4	Ti 2:13
Ps 119:74	Jer 29:11	Rom 15:13	Heb 6:19
Ps 130:5	Lam 3:21	1 Cor 13:7	Heb 10:25
Ps 130:7	Zec 9:12	1 Cor 13:13	Heb 11:1

Shame is a heavy feeling. When left unchecked, it can take root and form a distorted lens of truth. It's important to allow God to work through the shame—even when it hurts to *ride the wave*. Receiving His compassion and His hope takes away the shame.

> *"Go," he told him, "wash in the Pool of Siloam."* (John 9:7)

PASSAGES

(My homemade personalized license plate.)

In my pride, I want others to see what I see. But the Lord wants me to see what He sees. If I see the "I" as the Lord's, then it's completely different from being blind to seeing His way.

"Amy, do you see what I see?"

Put your name in: "_____, do you see what I see?"

What spoke to your heart today?

_____
_____
_____
_____
_____

Song: "Nothing Else" by Cody Carnes

Prayer: Thank God for what He has spoken to your heart today.

Look over life-work.

> *Do not conform to the pattern of this world, but be transformed by the renewing of your mind, then you will be able to test and approve what God's will is—his good, pleasing and perfect will. (Romans 12:2)*

Life-Work

1. Prayer for the week.

2. Listen to the sound of your voice.
    When you're frustrated or annoyed, can you hear yourself shaming others?

3. Look back on times in your life when you felt ashamed.
    What would God say about each one?

4. Read scripture, journal, and/or draw each day.
    On "shame," "compassion," or "hope."

5. What is God asking you to radically accept and/or be content in?

6. Continue to listen and validate.

7. Share next week.

It's an honour to share my story with you. Thank you for being willing to open up your hearts and share too. We're halfway through! —Amy

Shame

"Swirling, hurt thoughts, arrows of accusations. Something said, little or big—she can't stop thinking about it, and it's turning into a heavy feeling, a yoke on her. Bubbling into lesions and boils."

Compassion

"She's learning how to manage her time. Mommy, wait! Sure. Everything is fine."

Hope

"I have hope that God is taking care of me and my family. I can rest."

The Branches of Idolatry
What Gives You Shape?

SESSION SIX
Eyes on the Lord

Welcome back, dear friend.

Last time we talked about shame and growing in His compassion and hope.

Review

How was your week?

Did you feel shame, or did you shame someone this week?

When you had compassion and hope, did it change your perspective?

Did any verses or pictures speak to your heart?

Pray

Pray that you will listen and have an open heart for what the Lord wants to say to you.

Wrestle

This week, we're talking about *idolatry.* But first we will wrestle with the word "shape."

Who has shaped or influenced you?

_____

_____

_____

Who are you trying to shape?

_____

_____

    This word *shape* became exposed in my heart when I was told in one of our therapy sessions that it was my job to shape Nathan. In my heart, I instantly knew that he was the one who was shaping me! His actions determined my shape, then I responded with how I felt. With my *emotion mind.*

PASSAGES

I absolutely thought it *was my* job to shape our children, but I didn't have clarity, and it didn't sit well. Was it my job to shape my children? To God's Word! There was no shape list in my concordance, so I looked up verses on "potter."

> *For you created my inmost being;*
> *you knit me together in my mother's womb.*
> *I praise you because I am fearfully and wonderfully made;*
> *your works are wonderful,*
> *I know that full well.*
> *(Psalm 139:13–14)*
>
> *Yet you, Lord, are our Father.*
> *We are the clay, you are the potter;*
> *we are all the work of your hand.*
> *(Isaiah 64:8)*

What stands out to you in these verses?

_____

_____

According to these verses, who shaped you?

_____

> *Because of the Lord's great love we are not consumed, for his compassions never fail. They are new every morning; great is your faithfulness.*
> *(Lamentations 3:22–23)*

Study Notes for Lamentations 3:23

Jeremiah knew from personal experience about God's faithfulness. God had promised that punishment would follow disobedience, and it did. But God also had promised a future restoration and blessing, and Jeremiah knew that God would keep that promise also. Trusting in God's faithfulness day by day makes us confident in His great promises of the future.[8]

Reading that verse helped to renew my mind. In parenting, there are consequences, punishments that need to follow actions, but I don't need to be consumed by it. When I'm consumed by something, or someone, it is shaping me. And when I mess up, I don't need to be consumed, "... *for His compassions never fail. They are new every morning; great is Your faithfulness.*"

> *Train up a child in the way he should go;*
> *even when he is old he will not depart from it.*
> (Proverbs 22:6, ESV)

This is a catchy little verse.

Do you think it matters if we say "shape" or "train"?
_____
_____

What is the difference between those two words?
_____
_____
_____

Do you think you are supposed to shape your children?
_____
_____

Are you to shape your spouse?
_____
_____

Have you tried? How did that go?
_____
_____
_____

> *He said, "Can I not do with you, Israel, as this potter does?" declares the Lord. "Like clay in the hand of the potter, so are you in my hand, Israel." (Jeremiah 18:6)*

Study Notes for Jeremiah 18:6

As the potter molded or shaped a clay pot on the potter's wheel, defects often appeared. The potter had the power over the clay, to permit the defects to remain or to reshape the pot. Likewise, God had power to reshape the nations to conform to his purposes. Our strategy should not be to become mindless and passive - one aspect of clay - but to be willing and receptive to God's impact on us. As we yield to God, He begins reshaping us into valuable vessels.[9]

Amazing!

How encouraging it is to be reshaped into valuable vessels. That is incredible hope. The other option that seemed easier was to just sit in the mud and want the bad times removed. I felt paralyzed, as I didn't know if I trusted God to help me. I felt defeated, that I couldn't do it; it was too hard!

And that would be the point every time. Not in my own strength. He was showing me how to trust in Him. That it was in the mud that He would mold me, shape me, if I let Him.

Read Isaiah 45:9–13 together.

Study Notes for Isaiah 45:9

"A potsherd is a broken piece of pottery, essentially worthless."[10]

Any thoughts from those verses?

_____

_____

_____

_____

These verses feel like a correction to my heart. When I didn't like the shape of others in our home, or myself, I thought it was up to me to control, to shame and shape it out of them! Yikes! That doesn't sound nice!

As iron sharpens iron,
   so one person sharpens another.
(Proverbs 27:17)

What does it look like to sharpen one another versus trying to shape each other?

_____

_____

_____

Read Luke 6:43–45 together.

For the mouth speaks what the heart is full of. (Luke 6:45b)

What comes out of your mouth? Sharing is optional.

_____

_____

_____

_____

Chop—Idolatry

How would you define *idolatry*?

_____

_____

_____

The Lord was showing me that my shape was a core of what I believed and had my eyes on—exposing *idols* in my life. Sneaky idols, like the idol of Michael, our children, pastors, leaders, even the church. These idols took the rightful place of God in my life. Then I thought I had the privilege to not just teach and train but to shape those around me in my home, and that this was bringing me closer to the Lord. The truth was, it was pulling me further away from the Lord, and my eyes were opening to see my part in the fractured relationships with Michael and our children. I was filled with pride.

"... *human anger does not produce the righteousness that God desires*" (James 1:20). I felt broken and sad for the people I had put ahead of God. I didn't even know I was doing it. I thought it was out of love. I was deceived.

Grow—Eyes on the Lord

It took time for me to work through these things and gain His clarity, to have His understanding, and to believe it in my heart and *then* learn to live it out. In His grace, if I am willing to knock down my pride, He shows me another way, one step at a time.

What gets in the way of keeping your eyes on the Lord?

_____

_____

For some, a little pruning may be needed. For others, a whole branch needs to be chopped off. And for others, an axe is needed for the whole tree.

Read 1 Kings 11:1–6 together.

Study Notes for 1 Kings 11:3–4

> If Solomon, the wisest man could fall, so can you. Faced with such pressure, Solomon at first *resisted* it, maintaining pure faith. Then he *tolerated* a more widespread practice of idolatry. Finally, he became involved in idolatrous worship, *rationalizing* away the potential danger to himself and to the kingdom.[11]

Is there something God has exposed to you in your life that you have resisted, tolerated, then rationalized?

_____

_____

> *Because of the Lord's great love we are not consumed, for His compassions never fail. They are new every morning; great is your faithfulness.*
> (Lamentations 3:22–23)

THE BRANCHES OF IDOLATRY

Scripture

Choose a verse and share what it's saying to you, or you can do this as part of your life-work.

POTTER: one who makes earthenware pots, dishes, or other vessels from clay

Is 29:16	Is 64:8	Jer 18:1-6	Rom 9:21
Is 45:9			

IDOL(S): image used as an object of worship; false god

Ex 32:4	Is 40:19	Ezk 23:39	1 Cor 8:1
Dt 27:15	Is 41:7	Hab 2:18	1 Cor 8:4
Dt 32:16	Is 44:9	Acts 15:20	1 Jn 5:21
Ps 78:58	Is 44:15	Acts 21:25	Rv 2:14

IDOLATER(S), IDOLATRY: those who worship idols; blind worship or admiration of an undeserving object

1 Sm 15:23	1 Cor 6:9	Gal 5:20	Col 3:5
1Cor 5:10	1 Cor 10:14	Eph 5:5	1 Pt 4:3

What spoke to your heart this week?

_____

_____

_____

_____

Song: "In the Secret" by Shane & Shane

Prayer: Thank God for what He has shown your heart today.

Look over life-work.

> *Do not conform to the pattern of this world, but be transformed by the renewing of your mind, then you will be able to test and approve what God's will is—His good, pleasing and perfect will.* (Romans 12:2)

Life-Work

1. Prayer for the week.

2. What or who is shaping you?
   Take some time to reflect on what or who has shaped you in the past and what is shaping you now.

3. What idols do you have?
   If you need help, ask someone close to you what idols they see in your life.

4. Rest in Him.
   Idols are stubborn lumps to move. God has abundant compassion and hope for you.

5. Read scripture, journal, and/or draw each day.
   On "potter," "idol," or "idolatry."

6. What is God asking you to radically accept and/or be content in?

7. Continue to listen and validate.

8. Share next week.

pas'sage - the act of passing from one place to another

Idolatry

"Building own life. Collecting similar items to create own story. Controlling the environment without asking the Lord."

PASSAGES

Eyes on Jesus

"Jesus holding my world. Do not worry; take time to let Him lead the way."

The Branches of Self-Sufficiency
SESSION SEVEN
Confidence in Submission

 Hello, friend.

Last session we talked about idolatry and what gives you shape versus keeping your eyes on the Lord and being shaped by Him.

Review

How was your week?

Were any idols exposed to you?

Any more thoughts on the word "shape"?

Did any verses or pictures speak to your heart?

Pray

Pray that you are listening and have an open heart to what the Lord wants to say to you.

Last week we talked about idolatry. This week we're talking about the idol of self: *self-sufficiency* and *submission.* This can be a touchy subject. Don't shut your book yet!

Wrestle

How would you explain *submission* to a friend?

_____

_____

_____

_____

PASSAGES

I knew the Lord was speaking to my heart when I came across the word "submission" in a verse and had a physical reaction to reading it.

<u>Read 1 Peter 3:1–7 together.</u>

Study Notes for 1 Peter 3:5

"To Submit means to cooperate voluntarily with someone else out of love and respect for God and for that person."[12]

I laughed to myself, thinking, *So I don't have to? Because it says that it's "voluntary."* In the core of my heart, I knew that *I did not want to submit!* I was trying to understand from my mind to my heart, and then walk it out in my life.

Why is the word "submission" such a prickly topic?

_____
_____
_____

How does that word stir in your heart?

_____
_____
_____

<u>Read 1 Peter 3:21–22 together.</u>

The words that jumped out at me again were "submission" and "It saves you." I felt like the Holy Spirit was speaking life into my heart. When I submit to Him, it saves me.

Passages—My Daily Journal Writing

Submission ... kinda prickly. There is a stubbornness in my heart. I don't want to submit. Today in the testing department it is exposed that I do not want to submit. (I see, I said that already!) I really would like to go when I want and how I want. Submit. *Why is that my job too? Why don't others submit to me? Does the mom badge mean anything?* Tested again and again today. Now on the hunt to gain clarity on this submissive business! This morning I felt enlightened when hearing from the Lord. Now, tonight, I am just mad! IYIYI

Submission—another round of "word search" in the Bible. Concordance, here I come! (feeling witty in my late-night writing). The list of verses about submission isn't too long.

SUBMISSION: Voluntary, yielding to another, accountability[13]

"Voluntary." Check. Read that this morning. So is it optional?

"Yielding." I thought I grasped this months ago! Yielding to Him ...

"Accountability." Don't quite get this one.

Yes, who is keeping my kids accountable when they don't submit to me? (I am whining.) They are voluntarily saying "NO." God, are You showing me that this is just like me to You? Yes, busted. I can be so childlike.

God is patient and faithful with me when I am so *up* and *down*! I wanted to follow God's way but not submit. Is that even possible? Feeling *"tossed back and forth by the waves, and blown here and there"* (Ephesians 4:14). This is an easy verse to say, but my understanding gets in the way.

> *Trust in the Lord with all of your heart,*
> *and lean not on your own understanding;*
> *in all your ways submit to him,*
> *and he will make your paths straight.*
> (Proverbs 3:5–6)

If you were writing this verse about how you are living, what would it say?

_____

_____

_____

_____

I would have said: "Trust in the Lord when I want, and lean on my understanding; in all of my ways do what I think best, and He should make my paths straight."

I was learning to trust in His ways.

Passages—My Daily Journal Writing

It feels like God is kinda mocking me, but I don't think that's His character. It's me still having a bad attitude. And it is "I" that is mocking the Word. Yet how am I having faith to live this out? I don't understand! And I can't in my own understanding. *In all of my ways submit to Him, and He will make my paths straight.*

How I feel God speaking to my heart:

"Amy, I know you're feeling discouraged. I know your heart. And I know you're growing at learning My heart. In My time, I make all things beautiful."

I don't think I believe that. I'm struggling to trust You, submit to You, walk in faith with You.

"I know, Amy. As I guide you, know it is out of love, always out of love."

Today was hard. Where were You in me?

"Listen to My voice, Amy. Are you listening?"

I know I say that to Wesley every day. "Listen to my voice."

Okay, Lord. Praying for faith to listen to Your voice. Trust in You. Submit to You. I love You, Father. I am not on my own. You are here. Praying for my branch of submission to start to grow.

Thank You, Amen.

Another verse on submission: "*Submit to one another out of reverence for Christ*" (Ephesians 5:21).

Any thoughts on this verse?

_____

_____

I had demanded that Michael change a, b, and c; I thought *then* I would *submit*. It was not based on scripture, just self.

Read Isaiah 61:1–3 together.

What stands out to you in this verse?

_____
_____
_____

Grow—Submission

How is submission beautiful?

_____
_____
_____

Passages—My Daily Journal Writing

A crown of ashes is not attractive. Now a crown of beauty—that's what I want. Submission is beauty. I have never thought about it like that before. A beautiful crown instead of a covering of resentment. Joy instead of mourning. Praise instead of despair. *"They will be called oaks of righteousness, a planting of the Lord for the display of His splendor"* (Isaiah 61:3b). Such a fullness in my heart and belly.

Lord, I know I'm going to be tested in this … and You are gentle. I pray my roots will grow deeper in You. I feel corrected in my heart. That my roots don't need to grow deeper; they are already in Him. In Him, is in Him. The roots grow as the tree grows. I am an active participant in this. Growing requires submission to Him.

PASSAGES

Discipline

What is something you did as a child or teen that you were disciplined for?

_____
_____
_____

How did being disciplined change, or not change, your heart?

_____
_____
_____

Did you like being disciplined?

_____
_____
_____

Read Hebrews 12:7–11 together.

> *… but God disciplines us for our good, in order that we may share in His holiness. (Hebrews 12:10b)*

Discipline can be a touchy subject.

Describe a time when you were disciplined by God.

_____
_____
_____
_____

Chop—Self-Sufficiency

The Lord was showing me that when I'm not *submitting to* Him, I'm being *self-sufficient*. It hurt when this branch came off.

We have this beautiful tree on our property with two large trunks coming out together. For years I pictured that the tree represented Michael and I together as a married couple. It was a beautiful example of our "oneness." But then I felt the Lord showing me that it was my big branch of self-sufficiency. I had replaced my idol of Michael—well, not really—with the idol of self. With this branch chopped off, my heart felt super-exposed. I wanted to pull that big branch or tree back up to protect my heart, protect my ideals, protect myself from being hurt by others. My expectations protected my way of thinking. I saw that the idol of self-sufficiency was stealing His light, His nourishment, and the view of learning to trust in His way.

Reading Hebrews 13:17 opened my eyes and my heart. Many more tears flowed.

> *Have confidence in your leaders and submit to their authority, because they keep watch over you as those who must give an account. Do this so that their work will be a joy, not a burden, for that would be of no benefit to you*. (Hebrews 13:17)

This spoke deep into my heart. I felt that this verse was asking me to have confidence in the husband God had given me. If I am to have confidence that God has given me the perfect gift of Michael—not that he's perfect, but that he's a perfect gift from God—then I can have confidence in Michael as a leader of my heart and home. *"Every good and perfect gift is from above"* (James 1:17a).

I knew that I didn't have confidence. Instead of seeing all he *was* doing, I had been madder about what he wasn't doing. This is where it stung. In this verse, God was exposing to me the truth that if I didn't have confidence in the husband He'd given me, I didn't have confidence in God.

The study notes say that this verse is talking about church leaders. I felt the Holy Spirit show me that this is talking about the perspective I had toward Michael. I didn't like that.

I put my name in that verse to personalize it.

"*Amy*, have confidence in your leader *Michael* and submit to his authority, because he keeps watch over you as one who must give an account. *Amy*, do this so that his work will be a joy, not a burden, for that is of no benefit to you."

Insert your and your spouse's names. If you're single, put your name in with your leader's name. Children, put your parents' names in.

PASSAGES

When you put your name in there, do you feel joy, or does it give you prickles? Why is that?

_____
_____
_____

What makes it hard for you to submit?

_____
_____
_____

This exposed my heart to the truth that I wasn't submitting to God, and I wasn't submitting to my husband. God wanted my whole heart.

The more I read the Bible and became "more spiritual," the more I became hypocritical, bitter, and angry, and I saw Michael's lack of leadership. Joy? I sucked the joy right out of him.

"*Better to live on a corner of the roof than share a house with a quarrelsome wife*" (Proverbs 21:9). The rooftop was way more enticing!

My husband was leading in his own way, and I couldn't see it. I was so critical, mad, and hurt over my unmet expectations, so I continued to "puff" myself up. The Lord was showing me the impact of not submitting. I had my eyes on an idol, and the idol was myself.

I looked at verses on *confidence*, as I felt God showing me my lack of *confidence*.

> *A wife of noble character who can find?*
> *She is worth far more than rubies.*
> *Her husband has full confidence in her*
> *and lacks nothing of value.*
> *She brings him good, not harm,*
> *all the days of her life.*
> (Proverbs 31:10–12)

How does this verse speak to your heart?

_____
_____
_____

This verse gave me big prickles—again, with my heart exposed. I didn't like it! I've read this verse in the past and thought how lovely it was, or what an inspiration it is, or look at how well I reflect this verse! As I read it, God exposed my branch of *self-sufficiency* and my stubbornness about *submitting*. I didn't like this verse *at all*, because it made me ask if my husband had full confidence in me. I felt vulnerable. I felt like, "That's it, I can't do it! It's too hard! *And* I really don't want to!"

Confidence

What do you have confidence in?

___

___

___

What is hard for you to have confidence in?

___

___

___

What is God asking of you?

___

___

___

Can you see how you have lived or are living independently and self-sufficiently?

___

___

___

___

PASSAGES

I wrote a letter to Michael to confess to him my lack of *confidence* in him and in God. I wasn't sure how to share this new exposure. God asked me to be honest, and He gave me the words to share. I wrote it out and shared. I cried the whole time. My heart was broken, yet a lot of healing came from that. God was renewing my mind.

> *He reveals deep and hidden things;*
> *he knows what lies in darkness,*
> *and light dwells with him.*
> (Daniel 2:22)

This is part of Daniel's gratitude to God for giving him the interpretation of Nebuchadnezzar's dream. There is a mystery in each one of us: *"but there is a God in heaven who reveals mysteries"* (Daniel 2:28a).

Why does submission matter?

_____
_____
_____
_____

What is the fruit of us *not* submitting?

_____
_____
_____

What is the fruit when we *do* submit?

_____
_____
_____

THE BRANCHES OF SELF-SUFFICIENCY

Scripture

Choose a verse and share what it's saying to you, or you can do this as part of your life-work.

SUBMISSION, SUBMISSIVE, SUBMIT: voluntary yielding to another, accountability

Prv 3:6	Eph 5:21	Heb 12:9	Jas 4:7
Rom 13:5	Col 3:18	Heb 13:17	1 Pt 2:18
1 Cor 16:16	1 Tm 2:11	Jas 3:17,18	1 Pt 3:1

DISCIPLINE(D)(S): to punish, guide, entrust; punishment, guidance, instruction

Dt 4:36	Prv 3:23	Prv 15:32	Jer 30:11
Dt 21:18	Prv 10:17	Prv 19:18	Jer 32:33
Jb 5:17	Prv 12:1	Prv 19:20	Jer 46:28
Ps 39:11	Prv 13:18	Prv 22:15	1 Cor 11:32
Ps 94:10	Prv 13:24	Prv 23:13	Heb 12:5
Prv 3:11	Prv 15:5	Prv 29:17	Rv 3:19
Prv 5:12	Prv 15:10	Jer 17:23	

CONFIDENCE, CONFIDENT: being sure of something; without doubt

2 Chr 32:8	Prv 31:11	2 Cor 10:7	Heb 10:35
Jb 4:6	Ezk 29:16	Eph 3:12	1 Jn 2:28
Ps 27:3	Mi 7:5	Phil 1:6	1 Jn 3:21
Ps 27:13	2 Cor 2:3	Phil 3:3	1 Jn 4:17
Ps 71:5	2 Cor 3:4	2 Thes 3:4	
Prv 11:13	2 Cor 5:6	Heb 4:16	
Prv 25:9	2 Cor 5:8	Heb 10:19	

What spoke to your heart today?

_____
_____
_____
_____

PASSAGES

Song: "Thy Will" by Hillary Scott

Prayer: Thank God for what He has shown your heart today.

Look over life-work.

> *Do not conform to the pattern of this world, but be transformed by the renewing of your mind, then you will be able to test and approve what God's will is—his good, pleasing and perfect will. (Romans 12:2)*

Life-Work

1. Prayer for the week.

2. Talking to God.
    Write out the things that get in the way of you submitting.
    Ask God to show you where you're being self-sufficient.
    Give space to listen to His voice.

3. Discipline.
    Write out a prayer asking God to help you receive discipline from Him.

4. Read scripture, journal and/or draw each day.
    On "submission," "discipline," or "confidence."
    Read 1 Peter 3:1–7 again with a lens that submission is beautiful and life-giving.
    Does it change your perspective?

5. What is God asking you to radically accept and/or be content in?

6. Continue to listen and validate.

7. Share next week.

pas'sage - the act of passing from one place to another

Submission

"Submit your time to Me. Do not be double-minded. Do not let the enemy knock you off the course of following Me. I will show you where to go, what to do, and when. Just ask Me, beloved. I love you with an everlasting love into eternity! You don't need to decide today. Remember the sun (0)—sundog. I saw a sundog for the first time and was in awe of the look of it. I felt it was a visual way in which the Lord was speaking to me."

The Ice of Fear
SESSION EIGHT
The Melting of Forgiveness
The Fear of the Lord

Welcome back, friend.

Last time we talked about the idol of self-sufficiency and then growing the branch of confidence in submission to Him.

Review

How was your week?

Do you have any new thoughts on submission? Prickles or joy?

Did you see any branches of self-sufficiency?

Did you see areas in which you are or aren't confident?

Did any verses or pictures speak to your heart?

Pray

Pray that you are listening and have an open heart to what the Lord wants to say to you.

Chop—Fear

This is a hard one again. It's okay if nothing comes to your mind at first.

What is the first thing that comes to your mind regarding what you *fear*?

_____

_____

What can be the impact of fear?

_____

_____

Wrestle

I pictured fear like the results of an ice storm, with the branches all full of ice. Fear has a way of paralyzing and distorting reality. Fear was deep in my heart, and the thawing took time. As I reflected on my reactions, I was being controlled and shaped by my circumstances. I was assessing the situation through a lens of *fear*.

Passages—My Daily Journal Writing

The words from our psychologist at the end of our session were, "Don't be afraid." Really, don't be afraid? Yet I knew the Holy Spirit was speaking to my heart. Showing me that I am afraid.

I am afraid that I'm not doing a good enough job.

I am afraid that I'm not going to be able to be the wife I'm called to be.

I am afraid that I'll mess up this writing and not fulfill what God is asking me to do, as I'm not even sure I know what He's asking me to do. Okay, I do ... as I feel a loving reprimand from Him. He has asked me to trust Him.

Yup! Turns out I am afraid.

I am afraid that I've messed up my Nathan.

I am afraid that I'm not good enough.

I am afraid that I'm not really changing.

"Do not be afraid"

I feel the Lord speaking to my heart:

"Amy, do not be afraid. I am with you when you sit. I am with you when you rise. I am with you when you ski. I am with you when you feel like there is no one who understands you. I am there. I was there when you "lost control." I was there when you were "trying" on your own strength. I was there when you were knit together in your mother's womb, knowing the journey that you were going to go on. I am with you, Amy."

Breath comes into my lungs again. He is with me yesterday, today, and tomorrow. He is trustworthy when I am not. He is loving when I am not. He is gentle, faithful, creative, and knows how to connect to my heart, and He turns my sorrow into not so much sorrow.

I am led to these verses:

> *But Joseph said to them, "Don't be afraid. Am I in the place of God? You intended to harm me, but God intended it for good to accomplish what is now being done, the saving of many lives. So then, don't be afraid. I will provide for you and your children." And He reassured them and spoke kindly to them.* (Genesis 50:19–21)

Why were Joseph's brothers afraid?

_____

_____

_____

When I read those verses that day, I heard them from the perspective of God saying to me, "Don't be afraid." But reading it again, it's clear that Joseph is telling his brothers, "Don't be afraid." At that moment, I could see that situation through a different lens. Joseph was willing to forgive after *all* the *hurt* he had experienced in his life.

In my eyes, Joseph was justified to be bitter, angry, resentful, hateful, and vengeful toward his brothers—and angry at God for all the injustice and hurt he'd gone through. Yet he says, "Do not be afraid."

It would be interesting to have a conversation with Joseph to hear how he worked through all those emotions.

What can lead to fear?

_____

_____

_____

_____

PASSAGES

Are you living with consequences because of past hurt or fear? How?

_____

_____

_____

_____

_____

As I read this story again, I was overcome with the realization that my fear came from deep hurt. There was *hurt* that then led to fear. God was telling me, "Do not be afraid," and now He was telling me to forgive. That is powerful! In the flesh I am more likely to go with repaying evil for evil, or insult with insult. There is instant satisfaction in that!

> *Do not repay evil with evil or insult with insult. On the contrary, repay evil with blessing, because to this you were called so that you may inherit a blessing.* (1 Peter 3:9)

Any thoughts on this verse?

_____

_____

_____

This is what Joseph did. Years and years later, Joseph showed love and compassion. He was humble to his family. He repaid evil with blessing and inherited a blessing. Amazing! That is forgiveness at the next level—God's forgiveness.

We can be triggered by our deep hurts. When I was hurt, I was fearful, and in my fearfulness, I was destructive as I allowed that to fester in my heart.

Then the thawing began …

I reflected on the sessions up to this point and the branches that God was chopping off. I was able to see that each branch was laced with ice all around it. The ice was protecting my hurt heart, but it was distorting His truth, and again I was being deceived.

Going through the sessions up to this point:

1. I was bitter because I was hurt and I feared that I wasn't good enough.
2. My pride was a seal on my heart, as I feared my weaknesses and the weaknesses of others.
3. Through my judgement lens I thought I knew what was truth and I would respond in fear.
4. When I couldn't control the situation and the temptations that surrounded me, I was fearful.
5. I would take on the shame of fear and communicate with a heart of fear.
6. When my eyes were focused on idols, I feared that God was not enough.
7. Self-sufficiency, as my eyes were on myself, and I feared to trust in Him.

"Do not be afraid."

Identify a fear you had as a child, or in the past, that you aren't afraid of anymore.

_____
_____
_____
_____
_____

What other Bible stories can you think of in which decisions were based on fear?

_____
_____
_____

From our story of Joseph in Genesis.

Study Notes for Genesis 50:20

> God brought good from the brothers' evil deed, Potiphar's wife's false accusation, the cupbearer's neglect, and seven years of famine. The experiences in Joseph's life taught him that God brings good from evil for those who trust Him. Do you trust God enough to wait patiently for Him to bring good out of bad situations? You can trust Him because, as Joseph learned, God can overrule people's evil intentions to bring about his intended results.[14]

PASSAGES

> *And we know that in all things God works for the good of those who love him, who have been called according to his purpose.*
> (Romans 8:28)

Why can Romans 8:28 be a challenging verse to accept?

_____

_____

_____

The Lord was asking me over and over to trust Him and not be afraid. Yet when tested, I'd go back to my old ways. My eyes were on the situation and not on the Lord. I feared Nathan when I thought he was a devouring tiger. The truth is, he struggles with his emotions and needs me to walk alongside him. "Do not be afraid." The Lord was renewing my mind.

I felt the Lord correcting my heart with Michael. I feared that I wouldn't get my way. Truthfully, it's not for me to change him at all, as I'm not God.

I felt a strong correction from God: "Amy, get to know him for who he is today. You don't want to miss out on the *now*. If you continue to try to change him, it will be stolen by locusts, and you will be the one to miss out. You won't bring him joy."

I dove into the sea of *fear* passages to start fleshing me out and seeing His way. I knew I needed to be renewed!

Grow—Fearing the Lord

> *There is no fear in love. But perfect love drives out fear, because fear has to do with punishment. The one who fears is not made perfect in love.* (1 John 4:18)

How does this verse speak to you?

_____

_____

_____

_____

I had lived out the *love language* of fear, and now I saw that it had to do with the hurt in my heart. I would repeat 1 John 4:18 over and over again: "*There is no fear in love.*" He was showing me that He would help me trust Him.

> *Teach me your way, Lord,*
> *that I may rely on your faithfulness;*
> *give me an undivided heart,*
> *that I may fear your name.*
> (Psalm 86:11)

I have a divided heart when I'm living in fear. As I was going through my search on fear verses, I found more verses on *fearing the Lord* than the fears of the flesh. This was transforming and renewing my mind.

What does it mean to fear the Lord?

_____

_____

_____

_____

_____

God was showing me more of the beauty of fearing Him. It was freeing, comforting, and brought life to my mind and heart. God showed me how beautiful it is to fear Him. This was getting rid of the *freeze* and turning it into a *fountain of life.* Amazing!

My fear easily entangles. Walking in fear is not love. I could see that fear had damaged relationships, just like ice on a tree. Fear also kept me isolated, as the fear of exposure seemed even worse.

> *The thief comes only to steal and kill and destroy; I have come that they*
> *may have life, and have it to the full*. (John 10:10)

The last study note is from our story of Joseph in Genesis.

PASSAGES

Study Notes for Genesis 50:15–21

Now that Jacob (or Israel) was dead, the brothers feared revenge from Joseph. Could he really have forgiven them for selling him into slavery? But to their surprise, Joseph not only forgave them but reassured them, offering to care for them and their families. Joseph's forgiveness was complete. He demonstrated how God graciously accepts us even though we don't deserve it. Because God forgives us even when we have ignored or rejected Him, we should graciously forgive others.[15]

Any other thoughts to share?

_____
_____
_____
_____
_____

When I'm afraid, I lose His perspective. It's like looking through ice. I miss out on the opportunities where God wants to show His power through my weakness. I'm only trusting in my own strength.

Scripture

Choose a verse and share what it's saying to you, or you can do this as part of your life-work.

AFRAID: to be fearful or apprehensive about an unwanted or uncertain situation

Gn 3:10	Gn 26:24	Ex 2:14	Ex 3:6
Dt 1:21	Dt 20:3	Ps 27:1	Ps 56:3
Ps 56:4	Prov 3:21-26	Is 12:2,3	Is 44:8
Jer 1:8	Mt 8:26	Mt 10:28	Mk 5:36
Jn 14:27	Acts 27:21-24	Heb 13:6	

FEAR(ED)(S): profound reverence and awe toward God; and emotional dread of alarm caused by danger, timidly

Dt 6:13	Ps 34:4	Prv 8:13	Is 35:4
Dt 10:12,13	Ps 34:9	Prv 9:10	Is 41:10
Dt 31:12	Ps 46:2	Prv 10:27	Is 41:13
Jos 4:24	Ps 76:7	Prv 14:16	Is 43:1
Jos 24:14	Ps 86:11	Prv 14:26	Is 51:7
1 Sm 12:24	Ps 91:5	Prv 15:33	Mal 3:16
2 Sm 23:3	Ps 111:10	Prv 16:6	Lk 12:5
2 Chr 19:7	Ps 112:1	Prv 19:23	2 Cor 5:11
2 Chr 26:5	Ps 118:1-4	Prv 22:4	2 Cor 7:5,6
Jb 1:1	Ps 112:1	Prv 29:25	Phil 2:12,13
Jb 1:8	Ps 118:4	Prv 31:21	1 Jn 4:18
Ps 2:11	Ps 128:1	Prv 31:30	Jude 1:23
Ps 19:9	Ps 145:19	Eccl 5:7	Rv 14:7
Ps 23:4	Ps 147:11	Eccl 12:13	
Ps 27:1	Prv 1:7	Is 11:1-3	
Ps 33:8	Prv 1:33	Is 33:6	

FORGAVE FORGIVE(NESS)(S) FORGIVING: to pardon or acquit of sins; acquittal

Gn 50:17	Ps 86:5	Mk 2:7	Acts 10:43
Ex 10:17	Ps 99:8	Mk 11:25	Acts 13:38
Ex 32:32	Ps 103:3	Lk 1:77	Acts 26:18
Ex 34:7	Ps 130:4	Lk 3:3	2 Cor 2:7
Nm 14:18	Dn 9:9	Lk 6:37	Eph 1:7
Neh 9:17	Mt 6:12	Lk 7:49	Eph 4:32
Ps 19:12	Mt 6:14	Lk 11:4	Col 1:14
Ps 25:11	Mt 9:6	Lk 17:3	Col 3:13
Ps 65:3	Mt 18:21	Lk 23:34	Heb 9:22
Ps 78:38	Mt 26:28	Lk 24:47	1 Jn 1:9
Ps 79:9	Mk 1:4	Acts 5:31	

PASSAGES

What spoke to your heart today?

_____

_____

_____

_____

_____

Song: "Something Has to Break" by Red Rocks Worship

Prayer: Thank God for what He has shown your heart today.

Look over life-work.

> *"Do not conform to the pattern of this world, but be transformed by the renewing of your mind, then you will be able to test and approve what God's will is—his good, pleasing and perfect will."* (Romans 12:2)

Life-Work

1. Prayer for the week.

2. Is God saying anything to you? "Do not be afraid."
   Write out any fears that come to your mind throughout the week, and then write out His truth to each one.

3. Forgiveness.
   Ask God to show you areas of unforgiveness in your heart.

4. Read scripture, journal and/or draw each day.
   On "afraid," "fear," or "forgiveness."

5. What is God asking you to radically accept and/or be content in?

6. Continue to listen and validate.

7. Share next week.

pas'sage - the act of passing from one place to another

Fear

"What are your plans for me, God? What do you want me to do? What do you want me to say? (Fear of missing out/losing my place.) Peace and joy in resting in His presence and plans. The world rushes past; I'm ok. Dome/hedge of protection. 'Let the Lord's love for you shine in you and out of you.' PEACE."

The Soil of Jealousy
SESSION NINE
He Is Jealous for Me

 Almost finished, friend!
Last week we talked about our fears, forgiveness, and fearing the Lord.

Review

How was your week?

Did any fears come to your mind this past week?

Did you gain more understanding of what it means to fear the Lord?

Did any verses or pictures speak to your heart?

Pray

Pray that you will listen and have an open heart to what the Lord wants to say to you.

Chop—Jealousy

How would you describe jealousy?

_____
_____
_____
_____

What is the first thing that comes to your mind that you have been or are jealous of?

_____
_____
_____

PASSAGES

Jealousy has been a theme in my heart ever since I can remember. In kindergarten, I wanted to keep my best friend all to myself. Over the years, she'd often find a new best friend. Then jealousy filtered into our marriage. I was jealous of Michael's time, because I wasn't getting what I wanted.

Then the Lord showed me my heart of jealousy as our kids started leaving the house. I felt God was showing me that jealousy is like the soil my tree grew in, which nourished bitterness and resentment. I looked at the definition of "jealousy" in my Bible: "apprehensive of the loss of another's affection, vigilant in guarding something, feelings of envy or bitterness."[16]

Check, check, and check. That spoke to my heart.

This week's heart search is hard on the heart.

How has your jealousy impacted you?

_____

_____

_____

How has your jealousy impacted others?

_____

_____

_____

What is the rotten fruit of jealousy?

_____

_____

_____

<u>Read Genesis 3:1–7 together.</u>

How did the enemy plant a seed of jealousy in Eve?

_____

_____

_____

THE SOIL OF JEALOUSY

What happened when Eve's eyes went off the Lord?

_____

_____

_____

What were the consequences of her actions?

_____

_____

_____

What other examples in the Bible can you think of where jealousy led to the wrong actions?

_____

_____

_____

_____

> *Brothers and sisters, I could not address you as people who live by the Spirit but as people who are still worldly—mere infants in Christ. I gave you milk, not solid food, for you were not yet ready for it. Indeed, you are still not ready. You are still worldly. For since there is jealousy and quarreling among you, are you not worldly? Are you not acting like mere humans?* (1 Corinthians 3:1–3)

Any thoughts from these verses?

_____

_____

_____

When I see my kids quarreling, this verse opens my eyes to the posture of jealousy that is causing the conflict. When I'm quarreling in my heart, it comes out as harsh words or other actions. I too am being nourished by jealousy that is feeding my mind and heart.

PASSAGES

The verses in the Bible on *my jealousy* exposed my immaturity and unhealthy soil. I could see the need—and God was asking me—to get rid of it.

Scripture

Take some time now to work through a verse on *our* jealousy and hear what God is saying. It may be helpful to look at the verses above or below to gain greater understanding.

JEALOUSY: apprehensive of the loss of another's affection, vigilant in guarding something, feelings of envy or bitterness

Prv 6:34   Rom 13:13   2 Cor 12:20   Gal 5:20
Song 8:6   1 Cor 3:3

Write out a verse that stood out to you and explain why.

_____
_____
_____
_____

What would your marriage or other relationships look like if your jealousy was removed?

_____
_____
_____

Wrestle

I wrestled a *long time* trying to understand jealousy. It hurt my brain. In my mind, I wanted to feel justified. I wanted permission to be jealous. I wanted and thought I could have *my way* and it could still be *righteous jealousy*. Yet the Bible says: *"Therefore, rid yourselves of all malice and all deceit, hypocrisy, envy, and slander of every kind. Like newborn babies, crave pure spiritual milk, so that by it you may grow up in your salvation"* (1 Peter 2:1–2).

When we can recognize a bubbling brew in our hearts or actions because of our jealousy; it's like a big, flashing warning sign that something is wrong! It's important to be worked through. *Ride*

THE SOIL OF JEALOUSY

the wave. I had allowed jealousy to feed my heart over *many* years. Such a waste! As a friend said, "Jealousy—it's not a good look!" So true.

When I went through the verses, I discovered more verses on *God's jealousy* and learned that He is actually jealous for me! Wow, that's amazing! This was hard for my brain to understand, because I knew how destructive my jealousy was.

I've split up the list of verses on *jealousy of the flesh* that we looked at previously and *His jealousy for us* from my Bible concordance and dictionary. Take some time to work through His jealousy for you. Choose a verse and share what it's saying to you.

JEALOUSY: apprehensive of the loss of another's affection, vigilant in guarding something, feelings of envy or bitterness

Ex 20:4,5	Ps 79:5	Na 1:2	Zec 1:14
Dt 4:24	Ez 23:25	Zep 1:18	1 Cor 10:22
Jos 24:19	Jl 2:18	Zep 3:8	Jas 4:4-6

Write out the verse that stood out to you and why.

_____

_____

_____

_____

What makes God jealous?

_____

_____

_____

_____

Is it hard for you to accept that God is jealous for you? Why is that?

_____

_____

_____

PASSAGES

How does it make you feel when you hear that God is jealous for you?

_____

_____

_____

God was opening my eyes and showing me that He is absolutely jealous for me. He wants my whole heart, without any other idols in my life. That warmed my heart and was comforting. God was showing me that I wasn't to be jealous of my husband, friends, or our kids' lives. In my mind, I was thinking, *What about me?* I could hear Him say, "It's all about Me in you, Amy." He was renewing my mind and refining my soil.

Grow—His Jealousy

Is it possible to have healthy or godly jealousy?

_____

_____

_____

_____

I had confidently thought no, because I could clearly see that my jealousy stunk. And I was in awe and amazed that God would be jealous for me. I understood that I am *not* in the place of God, so there is no such thing as healthy or godly jealousy that I can have. I thought this session was done!

I re-read my personal journal from the previous year, as I was wrestling through a list of verses on purity. This verse stood out to me sharply: "*I am jealous for you with a godly jealousy*" (2 Corinthians 11:2a). This verse was not on my concordance list. Wait, I can have godly jealousy? There is such a thing?

Read 2 Corinthians 11:1–4 together.

Study Notes for 2 Corinthians 11:2

"Paul was anxious that the church's love should be for Christ alone, just as a pure virgin saves her love for one man only. By 'virgin' he meant one who was unaffected by false doctrine."[17]

The cross reference from 2 Corinthians 11:2 is Hosea 2:19:

I will betroth you to me forever;
I will betroth you in righteousness and justice,
in love and compassion.
I will betroth you in faithfulness,
and you will acknowledge the Lord.
(Hosea 2:19)

Study Notes from the Beginning of Hosea

Hosea highlights the parallels between his relationship with Gomer and God's relationship with the nation of Israel. Although the people made a covenant with the one true God, they went after false gods. In the same way, Hosea married Gomer, knowing ahead of time that she would leave him. Hosea tenderly dealt with his wife in spite of her sin. And God was merciful toward the people of Israel despite their sins. God has not changed; He is still merciful and forgiving.[18]

In 2 Corinthians 11:2, Paul writes about a godly jealousy that he has for the people, as he doesn't want them to be led astray by false teachings. Hosea had a steadfast, godly jealousy for his wife, Gomer, who had cheated on him multiple times and had children with other men. If I have a godly jealousy like Hosea or Paul, it's filled with God's love, compassion, and faithfulness. And because of that, *"you will acknowledge the Lord."* Others will be able to see the Lord! That is amazing.

What other stories in the Bible provide examples of godly jealousy?

_____

_____

_____

PASSAGES

What is the fruit of godly jealousy?

_____

_____

_____

_____

This perspective changes how I am to respond when tempted with *my* jealousy, which fuels resentment, bitterness, or other not-so-beautiful things that can creep in. Only in *His* strength can I have godly jealousy filled with compassion, love, and faithfulness to Him. That leads to His righteousness. This took me a long time to grow in His understanding. And it will take the rest of my life to learn how, to live it out.

What spoke to your heart today?

_____

_____

_____

_____

_____

Song: "How He Loves Us" by Shane & Shane

Prayer: Thank God for what He has shown your heart today.

Look over life-work.

> *Do not conform to the pattern of this world, but be transformed by the renewing of your mind, then you will be able to test and approve what God's will is—his good, pleasing and perfect will.* (Romans 12:2)

Life-Work

1. Prayer for the week.

2. Create a timeline.
    Where has jealousy been a part of your life?

3. Write.
    Take some time to write out God's love letter to you, about His jealousy for you.

4. Reflect on an area of jealousy in your life. Describe the impact it's having on you and others.
    If you had godly jealousy, how would that change things?

5. Read scripture, journal, and/or draw each day.
    On "jealousy."

6. What is God asking you to radically accept and/or be content in?

7. Continue to listen and validate.

8. Share next week.

pas'sage - the act of passing from one place to another

Jealousy: 1 Corinthians 7:17

"Wear my own shoes. "Do not focus on the world—look at Me. The waves are crashing. Eyes on Me, child. You are different. You are unique. Wear your own shoes."

Hate
SESSION TEN
With an Overflow of Love

 Welcome back, friend, for Session Ten!
Last session, we talked about our jealousy, God's jealousy for us, and godly jealousy.

Review

How was your week?

Did you see areas of jealousy in your life?

Did you write a letter from God to yourself?

Has knowing that God is jealous for you changed your perspective?

Any more thoughts on godly jealousy?

Did any verses or pictures speak to your heart?

Pray

Pray that you will listen and have an open heart to what the Lord wants to say to you.

Chop, Wrestle, and Grow—Hate and Love

This week we're talking about *hate* and *love* and reflecting on where you've been through this study. We'll also take communion together, if you feel comfortable with that.

How would you describe hate?

_____
_____
_____
_____
_____

PASSAGES

What are things that you hate? What gets your goat?

_____
_____
_____

Reflecting on Where We Have Been

As I shared at the beginning, I had a plank in my eye, thinking that everyone else around me needed to change. With Romans 12:2 on my windowsill, the Lord started to open my eyes to how I had conformed to the patterns of the world and not to Him.

> *Do not conform to the pattern of this world, but be transformed by the renewing of your mind. Then you will be able to test and approve what God's will is—his good, pleasing and perfect will.* (Romans 12:2)

Throughout our journey together:

Can you see any *patterns of this world* that you have conformed to?

_____
_____
_____
_____

Can you see any areas in your life where *your mind has been renewed*?

_____
_____
_____
_____

The first thing God showed me when I started on this journey was that I needed to listen more and do less talking. Most importantly, I needed to listen to Him.

From Session One:

> *My dear brothers and sisters, take note of this: Everyone should be quick to listen, slow to speak and slow to become angry, because human anger does not produce the righteousness that God desires. Therefore, get rid of all moral filth and the evil that is so prevalent and humbly accept the word planted in you, which can save you.* (James 1:19–21)

What obstacles get in the way of listening?

_____
_____
_____
_____

What difference does it make when you are listening?

_____
_____
_____

God showed me the moral filth and evil I needed to get rid of. *My* patterns were not the Lord's patterns. I felt justified with my attitude of bitterness, judgement, and the desire to have a leash of control. Communicating through shame, I looked to idols and grew in self-sufficiency. I was paralyzed in fear, with the soil of jealousy nourishing each branch. I had thought I was loving, but this all led to *hate*.

> *Therefore, since we are surrounded by such a great cloud of witnesses, let us throw off everything that hinders and the sin that so easily entangles. And let us run with perseverance the race marked out for us.* (Hebrews 12:1)

Sin easily entangles, like a snarly fishing line. When my eyes were able to see, I realized the impact it was having not just on me but on those around me. The Lord asked me to "throw it off!" I would resist every time—pout, rant, cry, and really act like a child. Through this journey, I was gradually learning to trust in Him and His way. I will continue to work on this for the rest of my life.

> *My sacrifice, O God, is a broken spirit;*
> *a broken and contrite heart*
> *you, God, will not despise.*
> (Psalm 51:17)

I had to look up the word *contrite*. Webster's New Collegiate Dictionary (1959) defines it as:
1. Broken down with sorrow for sin; humbly and thoroughly penitent
2. Proceeding from sincere repentance

Then I had to look up *penitent* in the same dictionary:
1. One who repents of sin

Wow, that is beautiful! This is where He wants my heart to be. Contrite.

How does it change our perspective if we have a contrite heart for our sins?

_____

_____

_____

_____

The discipline from the Lord, the chopping of our branches and having our planks removed, *hurts*! Then to see the sin in our lives and *hate* it is life changing. To be broken in spirit and have a contrite heart is transformation.

> *And let us run with perseverance the race marked out for us.*
> (Hebrews 12:1b)

This is a lifelong journey.

> *I say to the Lord, "You are my Lord;*
> *Apart from you I have no good thing."*
> (Psalm 16:2)

It's important to recognize that there is no good thing in me apart from Him. I need to hate sin and evil and then grow in the understanding that I am loved and you are loved. Then I need to live that out in Him. If I hate it, then why do I keep going back to my old ways?

Read Romans 7:15–20 together.

This is a hard read. Maturing is really hard. Growing is hard, and it's hard to change! It's easier to say, "This isn't working" or "I can't do this!"

Name something you want to do but don't.

_____
_____
_____

What is something you do but don't want to do?

_____
_____
_____

Read 1 Corinthians 13 (the love chapter) together.

What stands out to you in this passage?

_____
_____
_____
_____

It's a high calling to love this way. Without knowing, seeing, understanding, and hating my sin, I could not love well and would "*gain nothing*."

Only in God can I love in His way. When I am listening, He shows me how to see His strength in my and other's weaknesses. I then began to grow in His sound judgement, self-control, compassion, and hope. I'm learning to have my eyes on the Lord, with confidence that I serve the one true God. I'm learning that I am not on my own and that submitting to Him is a beautiful thing. I'm learning to fear the Lord and know that He is 100 per cent jealous for me. And through Him, I can love and learn to hate the sin that so easily entangled me and left me shattered on the ground with no hope.

Only God.

PASSAGES

Communion

Follow God's example, therefore, as dearly loved children and walk in the way of love, just as Christ loved us and gave himself up for us as a fragrant offering and sacrifice to God. (Ephesians 5:1–2)

Following an Easter Sunday as our family was sitting around the table after church, I asked our eldest son what he took away from the message we just heard. He said that he appreciated when the pastor noted that is was his 23rd Easter believing this beautiful story. Our son shared how it was at Easter the previous year, for the first time, Jesus' death and resurrection truly meant something to him.

Describe one of the first time(s) when you understood and believed in the love that Jesus has for you.

_____

_____

_____

_____

And He took bread, gave thanks and broke it, and gave it to them, saying, "This is my body given for you; do this in remembrance of me."
(Luke 22:19)

Take the bread and pray together, or in your heart, thanking Him, for the love that He has for you.

A shoot will come up from the stump of Jesse; from the roots. a Branch will bear fruit.
(Isaiah 11:1)

Reflect on your relationship with Jesus. Who is Jesus to you?

_____

_____

_____

_____

In the same way, after the supper He took the cup, saying, "This cup is the new covenant in my blood, which is poured out for you."
(Luke 22:20)

Take the cup of wine and pray together, or in your heart, remembering this new covenant, thanking Him for who He is in your life.

What spoke to your heart today?

_____

_____

_____

_____

_____

Songs: "Amazing Grace" by John Newton
"I Speak the Name of Jesus" by KingsPorch
"The Proof of Your Love" by For King & Country (Nathan's pick)

Prayer: Thank God for what He has shown your heart today.

Look at this week's life-work.

Thank you for being willing to listen to my story. Our journeys aren't easy, yet our story of Christ's work in us is the evidence of the power of Christ. And that is the best thing we can live for.

From Your Sister in Christ,

Amy

PASSAGES

Scripture

HATE(D)(S), HATRED: to dislike or detest, often with enmity or malice; strong emotional aversion; detestable

Lv 19:17	Prv 6:16-19	Prv 15:27	Am 5:15	Jn 3:20	1 Jn 2:9
Ps 5:5	Prv 8:13	Prv 25:17	Mal 1:3	Jn 12:25	1 Jn 4:20
Ps 36:2	Prv 9:8	Prv 26:28	Mal 2:16	Jn 15:18	
Ps 45:7	Prv 10:12	Prv 29:10	Mt 5:43,44	Rom 12:9	
Ps 97:10	Prv 13:5	Eccl 3:8	Mt 10:22	Eph 5:29	
Ps 119:104	Prv 13:24	Is 61:1-3	Lk 6:22	Heb 5:29	
Ps 119:163	Prv 15:17	Is 61:8	Lk 6:27	Heb 1:9	

LOVE(D)(S), LOVING: strong affection, desire, or devotion

Gn 20:13	2 Chr 20:21	Ps 116:1	Song 5:8	Jn 11:3	Eph 4:2
Ex 20:6	Neh 9:17	Ps 119:64	Song 8:7	Jn 12:25	Eph 5:25
Lv 19:18	Ps 6:4	Ps 119:97	Is 38:17	Jn 13:35	2 Thes 2:16
Dt 4:37	Ps 23:6	Ps 119:132	Is 56:6	Jn 14:15	1 Tm 4:12
Dt 7:9	Ps 26:8	Ps 127:2	Is 61:8	Jn 15:17	1 Tm 6:10
Dt 10:18	Ps 31:7	Ps 130:7	Jer 2:2	Jn 17:23	2 Tm 3:1-4
Dt 11:1	Ps 34:12	Ps 144:2	Jer 2:25	Rom 5:5	2 Tm 3:10
Dt 23:5	Ps 36:5	Prv 3:12	Jer 14:10	Rom 8:28	Ti 2:4
Jos 22:5	Ps 45:7	Prv 5:19	Lam 3:32	Rom 12:9	Heb 10:24
Jgs 14:16	Ps 52:3	Prv 7:18	Ezk 33:32	Rom 13:9	Heb 12:6
Jgs 16:4	Ps 57:3	Prv 9:8	Hos 3:1	1 Cor 2:9	1 Pt 1:8
Jgs 16:15	Ps 59:16	Prv 10:12	Hos 9:1	1 Cor 8:1	1 Pt 1:22
Ru 4:15	Ps 63:3	Prv 12:1	Hos 11:1	1 Cor 13	1 Pt 2:17
2 Sm 1:26	Ps 66:20	Prv 15:17	Mi 3:2	1 Cor 16:13,14	1 Pt 3:10
2 Sm 19:6	Ps 85:10	Prv 17:17	Zep 3:17	2 Cor 2:4	1 pt 4:8
1 Kgs 10:9	Ps 88:11	Prv 20:13	Mt 3:17	2 Cor 5:14	2 Pt 1:5-7
1 Kgs 11:1	Ps 89:2	Prv 21:17	Mt 5:43	Gal 2:20	1 Jn 2:5
1 Chr 16:34	Ps 89:28	Prv 29:3	Mt 22:37-39	Gal 5:6	1 Jn 2:15
1 Chr 17:13	Ps 103:8	Eccl 3:8	Mt 24:12	Gal 5:13	1 Jn 3:1
2 Chr 6:42	Ps 106:45	Eccl 5:10	Jn 3:16	Gal 5:22	1 Jn 4:15-21
2 Chr 9:8	Ps 107:8	Song 2:4	Jn 10:17	Eph 3:14-20	Rev 2:4

Life-Work

1. The prayer of your heart.

2. God has a love story for you.
    Write out your story, your testimony of where you have been, where you are at right now, and what you hope for.

    > *"For I know the plans I have for you," declares the Lord, "plans to prosper you and not to harm you, plans to give you hope and a future."* (Jeremiah 29:11)

3. Spend time with the Lord each day. Mature and grow in Him in your life-long journey.

    > *"Then you will call on me and come and pray to me, and I will listen to you. You will seek me and find me when you seek me with all your heart. I will be found by you,"* declares the Lord, *"and will bring you back from captivity ..."* (Jeremiah 29:12–14a)

4. Journal and/or draw
    The Lord wants to speak to you. Write down what He says to you. Listen and go back and re-read what He has been speaking to you about.

5. What is God asking you to radically accept and/or be content in?
    What is God asking of you next?

6. Continue to listen and validate.

7. Share with others what the Lord has been showing you and teaching you.

pas'sage - the act of passing from one place to another

A note for you:

Thank you for joining me on this journey. He is amazing at showing us little bits—or sometimes it can feel like big bits—of His love for us through His discipline, as He is always doing it out of love. I am in awe of the work He is doing in our hearts, and I am filled with gratitude to the Lord and for you, for taking the time to come and sit with me.

> *These are the commands, decrees and laws the Lord your God directed me to teach you to observe in the land that you are crossing the Jordan to possess, so that you, your children and their children after them may fear the Lord your God as long as you live by keeping all His decrees and commands that I give you, and so that you may enjoy long life. Hear, Israel, and be careful to obey so that it may go well with you and that you may increase greatly in a land flowing with milk and honey, just as the Lord, the God of your ancestors, promised you.* (Deuteronomy 6:1–3)

What are you crossing? The impact is huge when we are obedient to His way and the "passages" He has for us. Going from one place to another. A new beginning …

Father, I thank You for the work You are doing in each of us. You are the best shaper of our hearts and minds. You are the light and the peace, and You shine light in the darkness deep within. Thank You that You are there to help us walk in Your ways, even when it hurts and is hard. Father, thank You for being a compassionate and loving Father. You are telling each one of us: "Go, cross over the Jordan with me. Trust me. Listen to me." Thank You for Your Word, that is alive, leads us, corrects us, and speaks life in and through us.

Amen
With love,
Your Sister in Christ
Amy

A note to the leader:

Thank you for leading and going through this study. I'd like to share some of the things I have learned from guiding Passages.

With permission, I encourage you to ask someone to pray for each person as they go through the sessions each week. Not details, just to be covered in prayer.

Have a tissue box ready.

Give space to listen and for the silence.

If in a group, ask individuals for their thoughts.

In the tenth session, give opportunity to take communion.

Consider including a letter to them, a note of encouragement, a prayer, or a verse.

The After Ten Party!

Pray about having a retreat after the study is completed. Keep it small or go grand! Be sure to let the group know weeks in advance.

On the retreats we've done, each person shared their story or testimony of where they have been, where they are now, and what they hope for. Each person shared a song that speaks to their heart, then we spent some time praying for them and giving space for the Lord to lead. This takes about an hour for each person.

Consider having a significant person from each person's life write an encouraging letter. It could be their spouse, a parent, or child. It's special to have it as a surprise.

Every retreat looks a bit different. One of ours took place in an evening. We enjoyed supper, a campfire, and a special time at the beach.

We've also done a day away at a participant's home on the lake. This was two groups together, for five people in total. Not everyone knew each other, and it was beautiful.

Other times we've gone overnight at a participant's B&B with groups of ladies as well as couples. This gives more space for good food, worship, each person sharing their story, and reflection time, depending on the group size.

As a friend was praying for me because of an upcoming retreat, in her prayer she said, "that the retreat would be carte blanche."

When she finished praying, I asked, "What did you say?"

She laughed. "You know, carte blanche."

I didn't know what she meant. We then googled the phrase. It gave us goose bumps because it was a word she never uses, and we knew it was from the Lord. It means complete freedom to act as one thinks is best, and that is my prayer. That God would have complete freedom to act as He thinks best.

Endnotes

[1] Webster's New Collegiate Dictionary, s.c., "passage," (Springfield, MA: G. & C. Marriam Co., 1959)

[2] NIV Life Application Study Bible (Carol Stream, IL: Tyndale House Publishers, 2005), 2088.

[3] NIV Life Application Study Bible, 2088

[4] All definitions in the "Scripture" sections are taken from NIV Life Application Study Bible (Carol Stream, IL: Tyndale House Publishers, 2005).

[5] NIV Life Application Study Bible, 2349.

[6] NIV Life Application Study Bible, 2332.

[7] NIV Life Application Study Bible (Carol Stream, IL: Tyndale House Publishers, 2005), 1533.

[8] NIV Life Application Study Bible, 1289.

[9] NIV Life Application Study Bible, 1221.

[10] NIV Life Application Study Bible, 1149.

[11] NIV Life Application Study Bible, 512.

[12] NIV Life Application Study Bible, 2102.

[13] NIV Life Application Study Bible, 2360.

[14] NIV Life Application Study Bible, 92.

[15] NIV Life Application Study Bible, 92.

[16] NIV Life Application Study Bible, 2332.

[17] NIV Life Application Study Bible, 1953.

[18] NIV Life Application Study Bible, 1394.

Bibliography

NIV Life Application Study Bible. Carol Stream, IL: Tyndale House Publishers, 2005.

Webster's New Collegiate Dictionary, S.V. Springfield, MA: G & C. Marrian Co., 1959.

About the Cover Artist

Dana Cowie is a painter who lives in Owen Sound, Ontario with her family. She is an oil painter and focuses mainly on painting the Canadian landscape and her community. She prays that her paintings will touch people in a special way.

www.ingramcontent.com/pod-product-compliance
Lightning Source LLC
Chambersburg PA
CBHW080543090426
42734CB00016B/3188